MW00614972

Ascent of the Eagle

Being and Becoming Your Best

Charlie Palmgren

Innovative InterChange Press

Ascent of the Eagle

This book is printed on acid-free paper.

ISBN: 978-0-9801536-0-6

Library of Congress Control Number: 2007941271

For Dr. Henry Nelson Wieman and Dr. Erle Fitz
Two great mentors, teachers, and friends

Acknowledgements

I imagine most acknowledgements are incomplete. So many people contribute ideas, images, and stories along life's journey. My thinking is a composite of many people, situations, and circumstances. I believe it's usually some mixture of certain decisions on my part, being at the right place at the right time, and learning the right lessons along the way.

This book — like its predecessor, *The Chicken Conspiracy* — is indebted to the life and work of my mentor and friend Dr. Henry Nelson Wieman. Since Henry's death in 1975, I've continued to be nurtured by his memory and writings. He taught me to be creative. Thanks also to George Prince, co-founder of Synectics, Inc., who taught me how to access my creativity.

I thank Carol Lischalk for her friendship, encouragement, and commitment. I've likewise been encouraged by Rob Reiche, Hein Schroder, and Sonja Nels in South Africa; Johan Roels in Belgium; and Keijo Halinen in Finland. I continue to be indebted to Stacie Hagan, my former colleague and co-author of *The Chicken Conspiracy*. Thanks, too, to my long-time colleagues Del Poling and Mike Murray for their continuing friendship and guidance. I'm grateful to Bill Petrarca, a friend and co-author of *The Greatest Good*, and his wife, Jane Strathman, both of whom have been supportive of my efforts.

Over the past two years I've been inspired by Drs. Gary Brown and John Ely, who challenge me weekly to go beyond any current level of thinking I might achieve. To long-time friends like Carl Puccio, Bob Berlon, Ron Page, and so many others, I can only share my appreciation for your inspiration and friendship.

It's impossible to properly thank my current colleagues for their work to make this book a reality. Special thanks go to Bill Pflaum, who not only has provided insight, but has used his skill and publishing experience to drive the tedious process of getting a book in final form. His wise counsel has smoothed the way. Heather Martin, colleague and friend, has been an indispensable part of editing and rewriting. Her experience, creativity, and energy brought a higher level of clarity and usability. I'm also indebted to Kim Snow, who has put the values in this book to the test in her own life.

Without Frank and Kathy Hollingsworth, this book simply would not exist. Their tireless effort, encouragement, and financial and spiritual support have been selfless and constant. Their generosity and hospitality have been exemplary. They, like the others mentioned above, have walked the talk and talked the walk. This kindness was extended even by their daughters, Torey and Meredith.

Finally, to Marian, my wife of 50 years: Thank you. You have never given up on me writing this book. Your steadfast love never ceases to inspire. Additional thanks go to everyone else in my family, who always encourage and support me in my work. I've indeed been one of the lucky ones.

Prologue

A man found an eagle's egg and put it in the nest of a backyard hen. The eaglet hatched with the brood of chicks and grew up with them.

All his life, the eagle did what the backyard chickens did, thinking he was a chicken. He scratched the earth for worms and insects. He clucked and cackled. He thrashed his wings and flew a few feet into the air.

Years passed, and the eagle grew very old. One day, he saw a magnificent bird far above him in the cloudless sky. It glided in graceful majesty on powerful wind currents, with scarcely a beat of its strong golden wings.

The old eagle looked up in awe.

"Who's that?" he asked.

"That's the eagle, the king of the birds," his neighbor answered. "He belongs to the sky. We belong to the earth — we're chickens."

So, the eagle lived and died a chicken, for that's what he thought he was.

Have you ever felt that unexpected urge to soar but kept your feet on the ground because that's where you thought you belonged?

Then this book is for you.

It's about making the choice to fly, to transform, even when everything in your experience and everyone around you try to discourage you from taking off.

My mentor, the late philosopher Dr. Henry Nelson Wieman, said we are made for creative transformation much like a bird is made for flight. And, just as a bird confined too long to a cage seems to forget the desire to fly freely, so we forget the joy of transformation if we remain confined too long by the monotony of our lives.[1]

Suppose the allegory above had a different ending. What if the old eagle decided not to listen to the chickens and followed his urge instead?

. . . One day, he saw a magnificent bird far above him in the cloudless sky. It glided in graceful majesty on powerful wind currents, with scarcely a beat of its strong golden wings.

The old eagle looked up in awe.

"Who's that?" he asked.

"That's the eagle, the king of the birds," his neighbor answered. "He belongs to the sky. We belong to the earth — we're chickens."

The old eagle paused for a long while in reflection. Deep within him stirred an unexpressed instinct, remaining only as a longing.

Suddenly, he knew. He knew that he longed to soar majestically, too. He knew he had a choice to make, a choice that would change his life forever. At that moment, the old eagle was determined to be who he was meant to be. He chose to soar.

As you picture the old eagle pondering the possibility of flight, you might sense in yourself a similar longing to soar, to become aware of your true and original self. If so, it's a good idea to map your route and check the flight conditions before you take to the sky. This book will help you frame your flight plan and get in shape for the journey. So, go ahead. Look up!

[1] Dr. Henry Nelson Wieman, *Man's Ultimate Commitment* (Carbondale, IL: Southern Illinois University Press, 1958)

Introduction

It was an exceptionally hot summer night, so hot that my father was planning to sleep outside on an old Army cot. Before going in to bed, I stood by his side in the backyard of our modest house, looking up at the night sky. It was mid-August. The stars cast a brilliance that would make Fourth of July fireworks pale in comparison. My father told me we were looking at the Milky Way. Then he asked me a question that would change my life forever. He asked me if I thought there was life out there among the stars. I had no answer, but the mere notion that there might be was exhilarating. It ignited my lifelong passion for exploring why things are the way they are. The door of my imagination flung open, and I was convinced that something "out there" was part of who I was inside. I felt intimately connected to the vastness of the universe and somehow important in the grand scheme of things.

Something was indelibly etched in my soul that August night. It convinced me I had dual citizenship and that somehow, I belonged to the everyday consciousness of childhood and to a sage-like awareness beyond my years. What I didn't know then, but have come to understand, is that all of us have dual citizenship. We all are connected to our present reality and to something larger, outside of our current comprehension. This understanding came as I traveled to five continents, working with thousands of people of all ages, cultural backgrounds, and ethnicities. From these encounters, I discovered three fundamental values that I believe are the heart and soul of our collective human experience. These three values are the pillars on which this book is based:

1. All people have intrinsic worth.

2. Satisfaction is a life goal.

3. Innovative InterChange leads to satisfaction.

Value 1: All people have intrinsic worth.

In more than 50 years of studying human behavior, I have been struck by how unfavorably people react to rejection. I have yet to hear from anyone that it doesn't hurt to be rejected.

When people describe how rejection feels, they talk about being angry, disappointed, and depressed; having a sinking feeling in their stomachs; being uncomfortable and dissatisfied. What keeps us from feeling good about rejection? What makes it so painful? Why do we go to such great lengths to avoid it? It's because rejection tries to short-circuit our hardwired sense that we are worthy. What in you rebels against being worthless? What insists on your innate value? It's not your environment. The pain of rejection comes when the external message that you're worthless conflicts with an intrinsic sense that you are worthwhile.

Why do we find ourselves mired in this conflict so often? In our culture, we have come to believe more in the extrinsic worth that must be earned than in the intrinsic worth we were born with, the value that no one can give to or take from us. We'll discover later that when we act from our original self, we experience intrinsic worth. When we act from our created self, our extrinsic worth ebbs and flows with the whims of those from whom we seek approval and acceptance.

Value 2: Satisfaction is a life goal.

If you dig deeply enough for the ultimate purpose of anything you want to do or stop doing in your life, you will find you're motivated by very few core purposes: happiness, peace, and satisfaction. Case in point: Think of a habit you'd like to break. Then ask yourself, "What is the purpose of that?" Keep asking yourself that until you can't think of anything further to say or until you're repeating the same answer over and over. I've done this exercise repeatedly in workshops over the years, and no two people ever start from the same place. But 97 percent of them arrive at or near the same destination: They're all looking for satisfaction.

So what's the big deal? Many conflicts arise from differences that, ironically, originate in a universal effort to reach the same outcome. We tend to differ in our approaches and strategies, not in our ultimate destination. In our attempts to experience satisfaction, we often behave in ways that block the fulfillment of others seeking their version of the same result. We reject each other's worth, and we all experience dissatisfaction.

Value 3: Innovative InterChange leads to satisfaction.

So the challenge of life is to discern how to live in a way that honors one another's worth so that we can experience our highest level of satisfaction. This kind of satisfaction differs radically from ordinary, temporary pleasures. We experience our worth and highest satisfaction through a specific kind of process or relationship. Worth is the basis for that relationship, and satisfaction is the result. The process is Innovative InterChange, the third value.

What is Innovative InterChange? Simply put, it is a process in which human beings are working together at their best. When you choose to communicate and transform using Innovative InterChange, you start with the idea that all people have equal worth. From that central belief, you are able to say what you mean; you listen to and value diverse perspectives; you're eager to imagine creative ways to solve problems; and you're willing to put in the effort to make this way of communicating a habit.

This book will help you transform through Innovative InterChange — a natural, four-phase process that allows you to communicate with integrity, think and work efficiently and creatively, manage change and differences effectively, and find the satisfaction you're seeking.

The roadmap

The three parts in this book build on each other, with the ultimate goal of helping you understand why you behave and relate to other people the way you do and giving you skills and tools to change behavior that may be getting in your way as you work toward personal and professional goals.

Part 1 explores the five conditions necessary for Innovative InterChange to work. The first and most fundamental condition is mutual intrinsic worth, the condition created when we understand that our intrinsic worth is equal to the intrinsic worth of another person. Experiencing your intrinsic worth is different from having high self-esteem or feeling good about your performance or status. You can accumulate more knowledge, experience, and influence, and none of it will add to your intrinsic worth as a human being. When you're not experiencing your intrinsic worth, you're vulnerable to losing sight of who you really are and what genuinely satisfies you.

Who you are, who you really are, is what I call the "original self." It's the self you were born to be and the framework on which you hang the experiences of your life. These experiences lead to the "created self." The created self, sometimes called the ego or constructed self, comprises the thinking and behaviors fashioned and reinforced by family, culture, and society.

The existence of an original and a created self doesn't mean we have split personalities or that we are duplicitous. Rather, think of the original self like a mannequin fresh from the factory. Once it gets to the department store, someone puts a wig on it, dresses it in the latest fashion, maybe even poses it and puts it in an elaborate window display. This is the created self. You can still see the original mannequin peeking out from beneath the floppy hat and giant sunglasses, but the image it projects is not entirely original. It has been constructed, shaped to fit into and reflect its environment.

Likewise, each of us is a unique mix of original and created qualities; we're individual and collective, personal and social. Ideally, we want to balance these elements of our identity. It's important to understand that creating an image isn't inherently detrimental. Blending in is useful for getting along in the world sometimes. It's when you start to identify more often with your created self than with your original self that problems can start. We do this because our created self feels familiar and safe; it's the self that gets applause and approval—highly prized commodities in our culture. But as you become less aware of your true identity, you have to work harder to maintain the one you've constructed. And this can make your life really stressful.

Making the choice to operate from our original self can feel risky at first, but ultimately, it opens us up to forming richer relationships and having a fuller, less stressful life. Being authentic with ourselves and others transforms us, allowing us to experience our intrinsic worth, which leads to the satisfaction we've been seeking all along.

The other four conditions we explore in Part 1 are:

1. **Trust:** The willingness to risk sharing the best you know, and the humility to be open and receptive to the best others know; the assumption that other people are trustworthy until they prove otherwise.

2. **Curiosity:** Exploring and appreciating new ideas, even if they appear to contradict your own.

3. **Connectivity:** Understanding that your brain operates by discovering and creating links between ideas and that your imagination builds on those connections to create new ideas and solutions.

4. **Tenacity:** The commitment, discipline, and practice it takes to make new thinking and behavior into sustainable habits.

In examining how trust, curiosity, connectivity, and tenacity flow from the experience of intrinsic worth, we'll explore why these natural occurring conditions, present in most of us at birth, were central to our healthy development. When they were challenged and compromised in early childhood, we developed habits that often take years to overcome; some of us may never recapture and cultivate them. As you read this first section, you can look inside yourself and ask where these conditions are in you and make the decision to revisit them.

In Part 2, we will study the Innovative InterChange process, exploring its four phases and how the five conditions in Part 1 are critical for developing them. The phases are:

1. **Authentic Interacting:** To share the best you know with integrity and to listen with humility, understand, and learn from the best someone else knows.

2. **Appreciative Understanding:** To resist your culturally programmed tendency to think in "either/or" terms; to look for the similarities and differences between your perspective and someone else's; and to be willing to understand and acknowledge the context of and value in both points of view.

3. **Creative Integrating:** To absorb the differences you find

between your perspective and someone else's and then to use your imagination to discover new possibilities.

4. **Continual Transforming:** To resist your culturally programmed tendency to become rigid, stubborn, and trapped in the ruts of conventional communication; to have the discipline to practice and develop habits that will lead to new ways of thinking, behaving, and being.

Part 3 is the "how-to" section. It takes you through the eight practical thinking tools and behavioral skills that allow you to re-establish the five conditions discussed in Part 1 and to communicate and transform using the phases of Innovative InterChange discussed in Part 2.

The first two tools help develop the Authentic Interacting phase:

1. **Intent Sharing:** To communicate your intent and your message up front with integrity.

2. **Confirmed Paraphrasing:** To listen with humility to a presenter's message; to restate that message in your own words; and to verify that you understand the message the way the presenter intended.

The third and fourth tools support the Appreciative Understanding phase:

3. **Finding Positives:** To find value in another person's perspective — value that may have been obscured by your differences.

4. **Integrating Differences:** To develop "both/and" thinking by converting "but" to "and"; to recognize that there's enough room for diverse opinions and perspectives to co-exist.

Tools five and six develop the Creative Integrating phase:
5. **Reframing:** To expand your frame of reference to think about a problem, situation, or goal from a different perspective; allows

you to avoid missing ideas, options, and solutions you may never have considered.

6. **Reconfiguring:** To step away from your problem, situation, or goal completely and to use metaphors and outside-the-box thinking to generate new ideas.

Tools seven and eight support the Continual Transforming phase:

7. **Repeating & Observing:** To practice your new behavior, and to catch yourself doing it right.

8. **Positive Reinforcing & Correcting:** The feedback you get from others and yourself that your new thinking and behavior are working; the ability to adjust when you get off track.

As you can see, the Innovative InterChange process is at once simple and complex. It requires you to transform a mindset and habits you have developed over a lifetime. Transformation will not happen overnight. Once you start to make these changes, however, you will likely realize how clear and basic — how utterly natural — the process is. The original self is capable of an on-going process of self-renewal.

Part 1

Flight Conditions

Innovative InterChange
Core Condition

In the Introduction, we talked about mutual intrinsic worth, the core of the Innovative Interchange process. When we recognize that all human beings have worth and that no one's intrinsic worth is superior or inferior to anyone else's, we're open to the life-transforming process of Innovative InterChange. When you honor your intrinsic worth, you're able to re-connect with your original self, the self you were born to be and the self that brings you ultimate satisfaction. In Part I, we'll discuss the other four conditions necessary for Innvoative InterChange to work within and among us.

Chapter 1
To Soar or Not to Soar

It was early on a hot summer day in Atlanta, and my neighbors and their daughter, Sara, were on their way to Six Flags for the first time. As they headed for the freeway, Sara was lost in anticipation of the day ahead. Which ride should she go on first? Which one would be the most fun? Many of her friends had been to the park already and had told her about the new roller coaster that looped, corkscrewed, and dove underground into pitch blackness before shooting back into the light at unbelievable speed. So she was eager and nervous as she imagined herself on the slow climb to the first big drop. She knew it would be a heart-pounding experience — and she couldn't wait!

Later, as she stood in line for the coaster, people coming off the ride walked past her. Some of them looked ready to go again; others looked scared to death and were saying things like, "You'll never get me on that crazy thing again!" Suddenly, Sara was in a mental quandary: Should she ride or not? Maybe it's not safe. If she got out of line now, she could wait for her parents by the water fountain and that would be that. The anticipation of fun had faded into fear for her life. "But it's just a ride," she thought. "It must be okay. Think of all the other people who have made it back alive. Besides, I don't want to look like a wimp." Yet, her dilemma persisted: To ride or not to ride? It would take an act of will to make the choice. Distracted by her indecision, Sara didn't realize until it was too late that the line had moved and swept her into the front car of the coaster. In her unresolved debate, she had inadvertently chosen to ride.

If Sara had maintained control of her decision, what would have been the authentic choice? It could have gone two ways, really. On one hand, she could have refused to allow other people's negative reaction to the ride turn her excitement into fear. In following her urge to soar, even though she knew the ride would be scary, she would have honored her ability to transform. She would have honored her intrinsic worth. On the other hand, she could have disregarded the cultural definition of what it means to be "strong." Rethinking a decision after we get more information can also be the transforming choice that refuses to let the world define who we should be.

By letting the line sweep her up before she could make up her mind, Sara allowed external forces to dictate her direction. The world will do that to us if we're not vigilant. When it does, most often we end up like an eagle stuck in the chicken yard. Those external forces aren't particularly interested in helping us soar. It's up to us to stay true to our original self.

Lured by the spotlight

It's not hard to see that if we're at cross purposes with ourselves, it's difficult to make any decision, let alone the right one for us. And it's virtually impossible to have the courage to be authentic and act with integrity. We're afraid to be who we really are and who we might become. So through indecision or the safe decision, we leave the choice to the crowd, which keeps us from being fully ourselves.

This habit of going with the flow starts very early in our lives, as we're urged to fit into the restrictive boxes of family, school, community, business, and religious institutions. The famous quality guru Dr. W. Edwards Deming put it well:

"One is born with intrinsic motivation, self-esteem, dignity, cooperation, curiosity, joy in learning. These attributes are high at the beginning of life, but are gradually crushed by the forces of destruction."

These forces of destruction lead our original self to believe it should prefer to be who others determine it should be. We're taught that one version of who we can become is the right one and that our worth comes from being a socially conditioned, created self. We get stuck in the vicious cycle of always needing applause and approval.

Entertainers often talk about how good they feel during the roar of the crowd and how quickly that feeling disappears when they read a scathing review in the paper the next day. The high lasts until the next rejection, and then they're off in search of something else to boost their ego. Think of how much energy this takes. If we put as much effort into the care and feeding of our inner eagle as we do into reinforcing patterns of behavior to gain outside approval, imagine how much more satisfied we would be. If we pay attention to it, we can always depend on our inner worth to be whole, to roar with applause for us. The world is fickle. The original self speaks with integrity.

Being and becoming

All of this is not to say that our created self is not legitimate; it's as much a part of our identity as our original self. We're both who we are at any moment and who we're capable of becoming in the next moment. It's in this being and becoming that we experience our original worth and our highest sense of satisfaction, meaning, and fulfillment. The key is to be aware of when our created self has taken exclusive charge. This awareness allows us to make the choice to get back to our original self and lets the two parts of our selves peacefully co-exist. It also allows us to focus on that "becoming" process, the transformation that our original self thrives on.

In my own life, I've moved from being introverted to seeking out opportunities to work with people on a variety of projects. Growing up, I suffered from performance anxiety — I feared the judgment of others. Today, I know the reaction of others is a statement about who they are, not who I am.

To become more aware of the distinction between our original and created selves, it helps to understand the difference between self-worth and the popular notion of self-esteem. The Germanic root of the word "worth" is werthan, which means "to become" and "to turn into." It implies a movement and transformation that starts from within. "Esteem" comes from the Latin root aestimare, meaning "to estimate." It involves external forces making judgments. And we often confuse esteem with worth. When we say someone is worthy of praise or worthy of respect, we're judging that person based on an external standard to which he or she has measured up. The worth of the original self is not based on any comparison with others; it's based on who we are and who we can become.

As we'll discuss in the next chapter, it takes enormous strength of character to choose to live from our original self. We have spent our whole lives shaping and perfecting our created self, like an intricate mask we wear because other people like how it looks. If we take the mask off, we risk losing public approval. Fortunately, all the positive and negative reinforcement in the world can't totally stifle our urge to discover who we were born to be and become.

SUMMARY

We're often afraid to be ourselves; therefore, we fail to be authentic and act with integrity. We become creatures in conflict with ourselves and others. While beating our wings to fly, we construct cages to confine our misunderstood urges and longings.

The old eagle's choice to fly was a choice to let go of conformity to the backyard rules and reach for the sky, permitting him to be transformed. This is not to imply that conformity is always bad.

It poses a problem only when it blocks awareness or prohibits the expression of our original self — because then we lose sight of our intrinsic worth and assume we're worthwhile only when we perform according to the norms, customs, and practices of others. The good news is that within us, the eagle continues to beat its wings, if ever so softly, in an effort to be free. Transformation and protection are not antithetical; they can be complementary. The original self and the created self can be harmonized. The question "Is there life beyond the stars?" can be reconfigured as "Is there life beyond our created self?"

Insight Questions

Personal Growth

When have you felt as if your life could be more than it is?

Think of some instances when you rejected the possibility of doing something difficult because it seemed far-fetched.

Recall times when you wanted to soar, but felt silly even thinking about it.

Relationships

Do you look for the uniqueness in the person beside you, or do you compare him or her to the social norm?

Around which people do you feel particularly energized or most fully yourself?

Organizations

How does your organization allow people to express their unique selves?

How does your workplace encourage and reward (or prevent) people for being authentic with each other?

Chapter 2
Soaring with Eagles on Chicken Wings

I had finished my first four years of college, and before I headed off to graduate school, a friend and I wanted to cut loose a little and spend some time abroad. So I sold my car and emptied my savings account to finance the trip, and we set out for Europe.

After working our way through Paris on what turned out to be very little French, we boarded a train for Switzerland. I was about as fluent in German as I was in French, though, and Paris had drained my funds more than I'd anticipated. So, when a generous family in Geneva invited me to spend two weeks with them at their picturesque chalet 6,000 feet up in the Alps, I jumped at the chance. Though none of the adults in the family spoke English, the twelve-year-old daughter knew some and was able to be my translator. Her grandfather showed me a number of mountain paths I could hike, paths laid down by generations of cows, sheep, and goats passing to and from the valley below.

Feeling confident after some time with the locals, I set out one afternoon on my own to explore one of the paths. Hundreds of feet above the chalet, I came to an outcropping of rock too tempting not to climb. About 150 feet up the crag, I realized I was out of my element. It was getting late, I'd disregarded the cardinal rule against climbing without a partner, and I wasn't sure how I was going to get back down — especially without climbing equipment.

Once again, I was ill-prepared for a journey. Obviously, I did get down — though how, I don't really know. What I do know as a result of the experience is that there are often vast gaps among intention, action, and success.

When we decide to act on the urge to be our original self, we still have a long journey from the decision to fly to the actual flying. Learning to soar — or to climb — takes more than good intentions and courage. It takes a radical change in our mindset, and it takes commitment, discipline, practice, and positive reinforcement of the required skills and behavior. It also helps to be a bit naive — the old eagle likely had no idea how much effort it would take to turn his chicken habits into eagle skills. If he did, he may not have had the guts to take that first step. Sometimes we just have to be willing to wing it.

Out of your mind?

Mahatma Gandhi believed that the journey from our created self back to our original self begins by becoming the change we wish to see in the world. We must be willing to let go of who we think we are. We must be willing not to be in our right mind so we can allow our minds to transform. The old eagle had spent years learning to act like a good chicken. And being a good chicken doesn't involve flying like an eagle, right?

How do we summon the courage and strength of character to challenge what we have thought to be right for so long when our identity is tied so tightly to meeting the expectations of others? We just have to look rejection squarely in the eye and start taking flying lessons. We may crash a few times, and it may hurt at first, but the bigger failure would be to quit before we even begin, to become a victim of our own fears. If you make a sincere effort to change your mindset, you'll discover that following the inner urge to fly brings with it an untapped strength and energy that can invigorate and sustain you through the inevitable trials and errors.

People you love and trust will try to discourage you as you start your journey. You can count on it. And certainly, there's some wisdom in it when your well-intentioned friends and family say to you, "Are you kidding? You can't fly. You'll get yourself killed." At the moment you decide you want to take off, you don't have the skills you need. Yet, you have to start somewhere, and you have to stick to it. Honor your commitment.

Leap of faith

I have a dear friend who years ago wanted to do something about the plight of the poor. He lived in a modest, suburban home with his wife and two children. But he felt he could do his best work if he moved to the inner city. It was a tough decision: They would be in a school district with a poor academic reputation, and they would have to leave behind good friends and neighbors. Then there was the financial insecurity. There seemed to be very little upside to making such a move. Yet, his religious and social conscience ruled the day, and they relocated to Atlanta. The risk paid off. They mastered urban living. They worked among the poor, helping them build homes, find jobs, and develop an even greater sense of community. It was a life-transforming journey.

My friend was fortunate to have the support of his family but didn't necessarily start out with the skills he needed for his mission. He could have given in to fears of what others might think or say about his radical decision. But he didn't. And in being authentic, in honoring his inner call to action, he found the strength and energy to carry him through unfamiliar territory. It not only carried him through, it led to the development of new models for developing the inner city. Many of those models are still in use in a number of cities around the United States and in other countries.

The willingness to be authentic is one of the biggest leaps of faith we can take, and the opportunities to do so are plentiful and difficult to grab. How many of us in the workplace, for example, are so hooked into looking like model employees that we routinely take on more work than we can handle or accept a promotion we don't really want because we're afraid to say "no"? There is an internal conflict between what we honestly think and feel and what we actually say and do. The consequences of saying "no" may be real or imagined, but the fear of them is real. It takes courage to see beyond that fear and make the authentic choice.

How do we know if being authentic will prove worthwhile? We don't. The difference between hunkering down in our created existence and taking a chance on following our inner urges is the difference between just looking at the beautiful peaks of the Alps and actually hiking them. Take the risk. Discover who you really are and can become.

SUMMARY

There is more than meets the eye when we decide to fly. It takes a major mindset shift to embrace transformation. As we recognize that there is an alternative to how we're living, we also sense and believe in an inner urge to be more. Then we need the courage and the commitment to follow through on our decision.

Some would say that such a decision is not for everyone, but I believe it is. Without such a decision, the longings of your heart will continue to go unsatisfied. While the cost of such a decision may appear high, it's relatively small when compared to the choice of remaining in the backyard. As the eagle might tell us, "It is better to have flown and faltered than never to have flown at all."

Insight Questions

Personal Growth

Think of a time when you had to face the unknown. How did you feel, and what did you do?

How do you handle those times when your intuition tells you to do something and you find yourself second-guessing your urge?

Relationships

Which of your friends encourage you to act on your intentions? Which ones tend to encourage you to play it safe?

How do you encourage others to follow their dreams?

Organizations

How does your workplace support risk-taking and change?

What happens in your organization when people come up with new ideas or make suggestions for doing things differently?

Chapter 3
Trust or Be Chicken

*John was remembering how his mother had drilled into him that he
should always be trustworthy in his relationships. She insisted that
trusting and being trusted were virtues. She said it would pay off in
the long run. But over the years, John had been taken advantage
of by a number of business colleagues who couldn't or wouldn't
follow through on their commitments, and this had cost him a
considerable amount of money. He was determined that his son,
Tommy, wouldn't suffer the same fate. So, one day when he saw
Tommy working a puzzle at the kitchen table, John decided it was
time to pass along a lesson he'd learned the hard way.*

"Tommy," John said. "I need to talk to you about something."

"Sure," Tommy said. "What is it?"

"Climb up on the table first," John said.

*Tommy was eager to demonstrate his athleticism; so he jumped up
and stood facing his dad.*

"I'm going to teach you about the importance of trust," John said.

"What is trust?" Tommy asked.

*"Trust is when you believe someone when he says he is going
to do something," John answered. "Here's what I want you to do:
Jump off of the table, and I'll catch you, okay?"*

Tommy stepped closer to the edge, stopped, looked at the floor, and then looked at where his dad was standing. He studied the distances for a moment.

"Dad, move a little closer." Tommy asked.

"Why?"

"I don't think you're close enough to catch me."

"Don't you trust me?"

Tommy thought for a moment.

Then he said, "Yes, I trust you."

"Then trust me — I can catch you from here," John said.

Tommy hesitated for a moment and then jumped.

His father didn't catch him.

When Tommy hit the floor, he fell forward and caught himself with his hands. The bottoms of his feet were stinging, and his hands burned a little, but he wasn't hurt. He was emotionally bruised, though, and pretty disappointed.

"You said you would catch me, and you didn't!" Tommy shouted. "You lied to me. You said you would, and then you didn't."

"When you get older, you'll run into people who will promise to do something and then not do it," his father said. "Trust is a risky thing. You should think twice before you trust anyone."

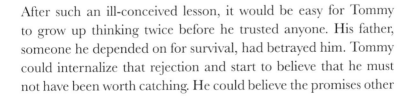

After such an ill-conceived lesson, it would be easy for Tommy to grow up thinking twice before he trusted anyone. His father, someone he depended on for survival, had betrayed him. Tommy could internalize that rejection and start to believe that he must not have been worth catching. He could believe the promises other people make him will likely be broken — so why trust at all?

Recognizing our intrinsic worth is the first and most important condition for the transformation to our original self. Upon that foundation, we must establish the second condition: trust. Trust is the belief that your intuition is worth following and the assumption that other people are trustworthy. Trust in ourselves and in others is fundamental if we're to start down the path of transformation toward our original self.

Survival mode

Like Tommy's father, every human being at one point or another will fail to act with integrity — the state in which what we say and what we do are aligned. We must not let this fact lead us into a life of suspicion of other people or ourselves. Trust is fundamental if we're to develop healthy, innovative, and transforming relationships, and if we're to discover our original self. The courageous choice for Tommy would be to think beyond the fall from the table and realize that he'll experience true satisfaction only if he trusts his own worth and the intentions and integrity of others.

Babies come into this life with a basic instinct for survival. They cry out for food when they're hungry; they sleep to replenish their energy; and they tense up until the strange visitor hands them back to their mother. This survival instinct is rooted in their DNA — their innate worth and trust of the world. We don't start to question this worth until we realize that our behaviors are falling short of the expectations of others. And because we internalize that disapproval, we construct a self that's more acceptable to the world — we pretend to be other than who we are. Being the self that others want takes precedence over being our original self.

We can't respect ourselves or anyone else when we're caught in this cycle of manipulation and deception. And without self respect, it's impossible to respect others. Mutual respect, trust, and courage are prerequisites for being and becoming more fully our original self and experiencing ever-greater satisfaction and fulfillment.

The business of trust

I once had a colleague whose definition of trust was the opposite of mine. He started out trusting no one. Everyone had to prove themselves trustworthy — guilty until proven innocent. I tended to trust everyone until they proved untrustworthy. (His approach was certainly safer than mine — his risk level was lower.) One could argue that, given the number of people in this world who are willing to take advantage of others, he was definitely smarter than me. But it always seemed to me that if I had to wait until people proved themselves trustworthy, it defeated the purpose of trust. When I trust you, I assume your integrity. I believe that the true *you* will converse with the true *me;* I don't need prior proof. You could say trust is more a matter of faith than belief.

Corporate culture is full of people like my former colleague. Quite often in highly competitive situations, people are automatically suspicious of each other. In the race for promotions and pay increases, people are frequently quick to share the bad about others and slow to pass on the good. In such environments, distrust breeds more distrust; performance and productivity are compromised; and commitment, loyalty, and morale tend to be low.

How often do you question the motives of people you work with and for? Do you think they sense your feelings? If so, how willing are they going to be to trust you? When we're mired in suspicion, we're focused only on protecting ourselves by shutting other people out; not a lot of work — whether at the office, at church, or at home — gets done. When we trust ourselves and others trust us, we have energy and freedom to be productive and creative. We feel satisfied.

Eagles seem so satisfied as they glide effortlessly through the sky. No amount of scratching at the ground or fluttering a few feet in the air will bring that same satisfaction to an eagle. We must learn to trust our own urge to be and become our original self, or we'll continue to scratch at the ground, searching in vain for meaningful connections with others and for satisfaction in life's little pleasures.

There is nothing wrong with little pleasures. We don't have to choose between them and life's deepest, most profound satisfaction. We can have them both.

SUMMARY

A fundamental condition of our original self is trust — trust in our self and others. Worth and trust are prerequisites for Innovative InterChange. Quite often, people who lack self respect find it difficult to trust themselves or others, and the failure to trust compromises our social interactions. If we always suspect that other people have ulterior motives, we'll focus more on protecting ourselves from potential harm than on opening ourselves up to the richness of Authentic Interaction. In relearning to trust our instincts to be and become who we truly are, we can choose to follow our deeper longing for satisfaction.

Insight Questions

Personal Growth

What makes it hard for you to trust others? What makes it easy?

How do you feel when you think people are relying on you to get something done?

Relationships

Do you tend to trust people until they prove untrustworthy, or do you wait to trust people until they prove they're trustworthy?

What makes a person trustworthy?

Organizations

How do people show their trust in one another within your workplace?

What would your organization have to do to increase trust?

Chapter 4
Does Curiosity Kill the Chicken?

I was watching a little girl examine her first jack-in-the-box. At first, she just turned it over and over, looking at the pictures and bright colors. Then she tried to put it in her mouth. (Who knows? Maybe it would taste good.) Pretty soon, she discovered the crank on the side. When she figured out it would move, she began to turn it — the box made musical sounds! Her eyes brightened, and a big smile spread across her face. Little did she know the surprise that awaited her as she continued to turn the crank.

Suddenly, with a burst of sound, the top popped open and out jumped Jack. The little girl was startled. She let go of the box, her eyes widened, and she stared at it for a few seconds. Then she let out a shriek and started to laugh. I pushed Jack back into the box and handed it to her. She immediately looked for the crank. She found it and began turning it. It happened again — Jack popped out, and the little girl burst into laughter. I pushed Jack back in, and she couldn't start cranking fast enough. We did this several times. She was fascinated by Jack's "Now you see me, now you don't" trick and the magic crank that allowed her to decide if and when he would appear.

The little girl was curious — curious about the colors on the box and whether it tasted like anything; curious to see if turning the crank and playing the music would bring Jack back. Her curiosity was so full and deep that each time he popped out, she seemed to feel the thrill as if it were the first time. Perhaps even more crucial than her raw curiosity was the fact that she was rewarded for it. Because she was curious, she got to discover and experience something new and exciting. Her world expanded.

Our journey toward the original self begins with a sense of our intrinsic worth. The second major condition for living from our original self is trust — trust in being our self and trusting others to be themselves. The third condition is getting in touch with our innate curiosity — the act of exploring and appreciating new ideas, even if they contradict our own.

Wonder why

How curious are you, really? When was the last time you squealed with delight at a new discovery? Over the past 30 years, I've talked to countless teachers, principals, superintendents, and education professors — and one thing most of them agree on is that as we get older, we lose the interest, perhaps the will, to explore. Parents, school, work, and our culture have eroded the curiosity we were born with.

As babies develop, they spend increasingly longer periods of time awake, most all of it being curious, testing their senses. As soon as they can, they start grabbing anything they can get their hands on so they can shake it, bang it, taste it, or throw it — whatever means they can use to discover it. So, how is it that we're born to be life learners but end up stunted? What squelches our curiosity so completely that we'd rather stick with what we know? The same thing that stifles our other innate qualities: the demands and expectations we place on ourselves to fit in with our culture. When we become what other people encourage us to be, curiosity becomes a threat to the self we've created. It morphs into caution and resistance to change. This caution starts pretty early in life, when we're especially susceptible to fears of rejection and punishment. We don't want to disappoint anyone — so we put away our jack-in-the-box; we stop putting strange things in our mouths; and we stop throwing things to see if they'll bounce because we don't want to get in trouble for breaking them or making too much noise. The point is not that we should actually behave like infants and toddlers; it's that we should be as infinitely curious.

When curiosity turns to caution, it's difficult to express our original self. That self longs to be more of who it's capable of becoming, but the urge feels threatening at the same time. So we become creatures of conflict in search of comfort. The main symptom of that conflict is stress, and we tend to seek ways to eliminate the stress by avoiding, suppressing, or medicating it. Curiosity is at the root of our innate urge to transform from a chicken to an eagle. We know this because when our curiosity is low, we feel bored, unsatisfied. There's truth in the adages "Familiarity breeds contempt" and "If you've seen one, you've seen them all." We need variety and change in order to be satisfied.

See you on the flip side

Of course, there are risks associated with curiosity. It often precedes discovery and change, and everything new is not necessarily better, right? Not all change is rewarded with smiles and squeals of joy and laughter — it can initially lead to unwanted consequences. But such consequences can lead us to our original self if we're patient and willing to seek the upside. Curiosity may kill the cat at first, but satisfaction can bring it back.

It's important to note that we're designed for a unique combination of change and stability — too much change, and we get confused; too much stability, and we become complacent. Being and becoming are two sides of the same coin. Both are required in order to be who we really are. The strange paradox of our lives is that we can be satisfied being who we are and who we are yet to become. This is the basis for our dual citizenship.

For our own curiosity to take us places, we must remember to trust and be curious about the differences we experience in others. Rather than being suspicious, cautious, and judgmental of others who think differently and make different choices than we do, we must be open to learn from them. We may be used to flying only a few feet in the air, but that doesn't mean we should mock those who soar.

SUMMARY

We come into the world full of unbridled curiosity. It doesn't occur to us to be cautious or not to explore new things. As we age, our world discourages and sometimes even penalizes us for stretching our wings, for experimenting. So we stop questioning and wondering. We settle for what we already know and become suspicious of what we don't understand or haven't experienced.

Curiosity, the third condition, is the basis for our learning and development, an essential element for discovering our original self and for exploring others and our world. It's a matter of keeping our inner child alive in the process of becoming adults. It is realizing that we're both being and becoming — always. So the real question is not, "Is there life after death?" The real question is, "How much life is there after birth?"

Insight Questions

Personal Growth

What does "Curiosity killed the cat" mean to you?

When in your life have you tended to do the most experimenting, wondering, and exploring?

Relationships

How do you encourage those around you to be curious?

When someone seems to be curious about who you are, how do you feel? How do you react?

Organizations

How is curiosity encouraged and discouraged in your organization?

What are the positives and drawbacks of being curious?

Chapter 5
Get Connected

Shannon was taking a shower. She was thinking about the things she wanted to accomplish that day, and suddenly, seemingly out of nowhere, she had an "Aha" moment. The answer to a work problem popped into her head. It was an answer she had desperately searched for two days earlier. "Where was that answer when I needed it? Why didn't it come sooner?" she thought "Why don't some ideas come when we want or need them? Why do they occur to us at random moments — when we're in the shower, in the car running errands, or working out at the gym?" She shut off the water, grabbed a towel, and went for a piece of paper and a pencil. She wanted to write down the idea before it sank back into the recesses of her mind.

Later, as she was putting the final touches on her eye shadow, she found herself wondering if there were a way to have more control over those "Aha" moments. She remembered reading an article the previous week about some research that revealed that the human brain makes connections during the learning process and that some connections fade when we don't refer to them for long periods of time. Then the cliché "Use it or lose it" jumped into her head. "That's interesting," she thought. "The cliché must be 'connected' with my thoughts about how the brain connects things." Shannon couldn't help but marvel at how interesting the human mind is and how little she knew about her own.

Like Shannon, scientists have long marveled at the brain and the way it operates. Some have suggested that the human mind is like a powerful computer, capable of associating and networking ideas, images, and meanings in endless combinations and patterns at remarkable speeds; some believe that our brains are capable of indefinite expansion and development.

So with all this apparent capacity, is it possible to have the "control over those 'Aha' moments" that Shannon wondered about? There is research out there — some studies of Buddhist monks, for example — that focuses on what happens during altered states of consciousness and whether such states offer us more control over our cranial computers. I would suggest that it doesn't require the intensity of Buddhist meditation to tap into our minds' natural abilities to make valuable connections. Like the other conditions we've talked about so far, it starts simply with awareness — an awareness that our brains operate by discovering and creating links between ideas and that our imaginations build on those connections to create new ideas and solutions. I call this fourth condition "Connectivity." This condition, which I also call the "creative zone," is one in which our original self thrives and where "Aha" moments come from.

Connectivity can be an individual experience, like it was with Shannon, whose past experience and the need to solve a problem were interacting and connecting in ways she had not previously been able to put together — consciously, at least. Connectivity also is an important condition of effective human interaction. When we listen to someone else's perspective and integrate it with our own, we connect with a different way of thinking and being. We get past our habit of one-dimensional thinking and are more open to integrating ideas that may have previously upset our well-honed perspective.

The process of making these connections is crucial in the journey toward our original self. When our eagle first saw the bird flying overhead, he had never flown like that, but he didn't let that stop him from imagining it was possible. His imagination acted as a bridge to enable him to connect what the bird in the sky was doing with his inner urge to do the same. In a similar fashion we must be willing and able to entertain new ideas, even if they seem to conflict with our current frame of reference. That's what Connectivity is all about:

We've established that embracing our intrinsic worth is the first step toward our original self. Second is trust — trust in others and trust that our original self is worth embracing. Third, we must be curious enough about life on the flip side of our created self that we're willing to explore and experiment. Now, curiosity through our imagination can connect us with other ways of thinking and being.

Un-stick your guns

Making new connections and integrating them into patterns of meaning seem natural for infants and young children. Just listen to preschoolers—they're constantly asking "why?" They're activating their curiosity; they're looking for ways to connect to the larger world. This curiosity motivates children to explore new territory: What happens if I push this button, or pull out this drawer, or eat this bug? And creativity allows them to forge new connections as they discover the answers for their questions. As adults, we have to work much harder to summon this kind of creativity. I'm not referring to the creativity many people associate with music, art, and literature. I'm talking about the creativity that motivates us to step outside of our created self, the inner force that pushes us beyond current boundaries toward new possibilities.

As we grow, we are caught between 1) our natural urge to make new connections whenever new information hits our radar and 2) our conditioning, which tells us to stick to what we know. Any connection we do make is fragile, vulnerable to disruption from a variety of sources. It's vulnerable because from our youngest years, the urge to become our original self collides with who our parents and society expect us to be. Hanging on to our eagle inclinations is not easy without the support of responsive adults and peers. When our innate trust is reduced to suspicion and our curiosity is reduced to caution, it limits our willingness to be exposed to new things and situations, frustrating our capacity to experiment, explore, and create novel connections.

By the time we're adults, caution can turn into full-fledged fear of ideas that differ from our own. We don't necessarily know we're afraid — we interpret our resistance as "sticking to our guns," as being principled, having conviction, and not flip flopping. In fact, what we might be stuck in is a rigid mindset that keeps us from entertaining new ways of thinking, new ways of doing, and new ways of being and becoming our original self.

Unlock the possibilities

Imagination is a valuable tool for loosening our mindset and reducing our resistance to change and transformation. Most adults don't use their imagination this way, but the ability is there. Unfortunately, when we do tap into our imagination, we often use it against ourselves, playing devil's advocate, assuming worst case scenario. Why not play angel's advocate for a change and assume best case scenario? Imagine what might go right rather than what might go wrong. How we use our imaginations shapes the kinds of connections we are willing to accept and reject.

How often in your work are you asked to use your imagination to come up with creative ideas that challenge the status quo? Corporate executives who talk about how they wish their organizations were more innovative could not only encourage their staff to use their imaginations, but they could make sure employees are not penalized for off-the-wall thinking and controversial ideas. There's opportunity in apparent conflict — if only the organization can imagine how the conflicting ideas might be connected and lead to new ones that could be more effective and productive. Learning to think outside the box opens the way to make many more connections. Our mental boxes limit the richness and variety of connections we're able to make personally and collectively.

We can make a certain number of connections within our current boxes. It feels safe there. We can also start making connections beyond those boxes — beyond the backyard. The good news is that when we do, we'll discover that the comfort in our current box can accompany us into the creative zone. We don't have to choose between being comfortable or becoming creative. Creative comfort occurs when we're at home with our original self. Lasting satisfaction, the satisfaction we're designed to sustain, comes only from the experience of being and becoming our original and authentic selves.

SUMMARY

Trust, curiosity, and connectivity are three of the conditions for engaging in Innovative InterChange. Compromise one, and you compromise them all. They're interdependent and reciprocal. They're present in infants to a greater or lesser degree. Genetics and our social and physical environments can all have a nurturing and/or debilitating influence on these conditions. Parenting, early childhood development, and early formal education have critical and usually life-long consequences. If your self-worth and respect have been damaged early, it's hard — but not impossible — to recover the creative thrust of your original self.

How can you allow yourself to be out of your mind so you can change the way you think? How can you return to a child-like freedom to ask lots of questions, to imagine endless possibilities? What habits do you need to let go of to overcome your fear of change and risk your comfort for something enlivening that stretches you? Instead of working to remain safe, stable, and in control, spread your wings and give your dream a try.

Insight Questions

Personal Growth

Think of a time when you were dreading a certain person or event only to discover that it wasn't as bad as you thought. What reasons did you give yourself to endure all that worry?

On a scale of one to ten, with one being unimaginative and ten being very imaginative, how would you rate yourself? Why?

Relationships

How would others rate you on the one-to-ten scale above? Why do you think they would rate you that way?

Think of a recent time when you imagined what others were thinking and decided what their motives were. Did you check to see if you were right?

Organizations

How does your organization encourage the use of imagination?

When and how has someone in your organization encouraged you to think outside the box?

Chapter 6
If You Pay the Price, You Can Keep the Change

Ben Hogan was one of the greatest golfers of the 20th century. By the time he retired in 1971, he had 64 PGA wins, including nine major championships. Ten years after his death, only three other golfers had beaten his championship record. But Hogan didn't start out blowing away the competition. It took him nine years to win his first professional tournament, and he reportedly went broke more than once as he struggled to master the game.

When he finally did make the big leagues, he refused to rest on his laurels. He always saw opportunities to refine his skills. One story goes that after a practice round in which he had scored a 64, which was well below par, Hogan decided he wasn't happy with the approach he'd made on one of the holes. So instead of reveling in his impressive score, he took the iron he'd used on the shot, returned to the hole, and proceeded to hit the same shot 300 times before he packed up and headed home.

What kept Ben Hogan from quitting, what drove him to keep trying, was sheer determination — the kind of tenacity that turns a birdie into an eagle. Hogan is proof that you can always improve. This doesn't mean you have to be a perfectionist. It means you can enjoy improving on your current best.

Tenacity is the fifth critical condition on the road to reclaiming our original self. We honor our worth, trust that there's value in pursuing it, use our curiosity to explore the possibilities, imagine new ways of being, and then practice, practice, practice to turn new skills into sustainable habits.

It's one thing to think about flying; it's quite another to be willing to practice enough that you actually learn to fly and stay airborne. We don't get good at anything without practice. Just look at toddlers learning to walk. They're tenacious. They hoist themselves up onto wobbly legs, take a few steps, fall down, and then repeat the process over and over until they can make it all the way across the room without losing their balance.

We, too, have to develop the strength and skill to be our original self. Imagining ourselves soaring with the eagle is the easy part. Actual flying takes a lot of practice. And you will have to put up with a lot of bumps, bruises, and strange looks from your neighbors. It might not seem worth it at first. But you have to be willing to pay the price if you want to feel the satisfaction of flying.

The biggest obstacle to being our original self is the comfort we feel in being our created self. We're going to have to let go of some old habits if we are to develop new ones, and forming new habits is difficult. This is particularly true when it comes to new ways of thinking. Some current studies indicate it takes an adult thirty to sixty days of positively reinforced repetition to master new ways of thinking.

Keep in mind, the old eagle doesn't have to give up all things chicken in order to master eagle flight. He can be both conventional and original, remaining friends with his chicken neighbors and taking every opportunity to fly high above them. It can be done — if you're willing to pay the price, you can keep the change.

SUMMARY

We have examined five interdependent critical flight conditions. If we're to be our original self, we must be in touch with our intrinsic worth. This is the cornerstone of the conditions. In experiencing our intrinsic worth, we're more likely to trust ourselves, others, and the world. We also experience our natural sense of curiosity and the urge to explore, experiment, and discover differences and similarities in other points of view. We experience our innate capacity to form connections and become more of ourselves through imagination and transformation. And then we experience our inclination to persist in both being and becoming more of our original self.

Insight Questions

Personal Growth
Think about the last time you gave up trying to master something or reach a goal. Why do you think you quit?

Why is it hard for you to keep working at tasks you find boring or monotonous?

Relationships
What do you think the key to long-term relationships is?

They say it takes patience to develop new relationships. Do you have that kind of patience?

Organizations
How does your organization ensure that it does what it says it will do? What is your role in that?

What can organizations do to increase the willingness of their people to do what it takes to get the job done?

Chapter 7

Talk Yourself Into It

It was 3:17a.m., and Phil was still awake, too hot one moment and grabbing for the blanket the next. The sound of the air purifier was usually soothing to him, but it was loud and distracting tonight — almost as loud as his racing thoughts, which were caught in an endless loop.

He couldn't stop thinking about the conversation he'd had earlier with his boss. During his performance review, she'd asked him how he was feeling about his job. He hadn't seemed very engaged lately, and she wondered if he was truly happy being an accountant. She asked him that classic question, "If you could have any other job in the world, what would it be?" He had no idea how to answer, but he had a feeling deep down that she was right about accounting — it didn't fulfill him.

"But accounting is what I know," he said to himself. "It's who I am. What else would I do?" His father had owned a small accounting shop, where Phil had gotten valuable experience during summers in high school and college. He had graduated with decent grades and a business degree from a prominent liberal arts college and gone straight to work for a well-respected firm. This is who he was meant to be. How could he consider another career? He'd have to start all over again if he left the firm. "Maybe I don't look forward to going to work every day," he thought. "But at least I know what to do there. I know what people expect of me. I know how to be an accountant. Now just go to sleep, for crying out loud!"

Suddenly, Phil realized he was talking to himself. And he was listening to himself talk. He felt like he was at war with himself. If he was telling himself he wasn't happy at his job, why wasn't he paying attention? Was he going mad? Why was he a victim of his own thinking, and what part of him was doing the victimizing? Somewhere in the midst of all this talking, he finally fell into a deep, but short, sleep. He awoke abruptly when the radio snapped on with a commercial for a new non-habit forming sleep aid. It was time to go to work.

Henry Ford said, "Whether you believe you can do a thing or not, you are right." The point is, how ever you think about and talk to yourself is the basis of who you are and what you do with your life. It shapes your self-image and your perspective. So, if we're going to reach this goal of living from our original self instead of our created self, we must think about and talk to ourselves differently. To change our deeply engrained self-talk takes all the conditions we've talked about so far: positive self regard, trust, curiosity, imagination, and a lot of tenacity.

If Phil is going to find peace in his professional life, he'll have to change the way he talks to himself. He'll have to let go of the mantra "Accounting is what I know. It's what I do. It's who I am."

Before we can change our self-talk, we have to become aware of it. How do you become conscious of your internal dialogue? Try this: As you move through the day, simply observe what you're thinking, and then say to yourself, "I have thoughts, but I'm not only my thoughts." Observe your emotions, and then say, "I have emotions, but I'm not only my emotions." Observe some of the things you do, and then say, "I do things, but I'm not only the things I do." Once we free ourselves from the notion that we're only what we've told ourselves we are, we begin to say different things to ourselves — we imagine ourselves in new ways and start the process of becoming more of who we're capable of becoming.

Don't worry — you don't have to change your self-talk all at once. Your conventional conversation has been going on for a long time, and it won't turn on a dime. It'll be a gradual process. Our eagle started slowly. First, he simply paid attention to the tug he felt when he saw the other bird flying overhead. It was his original self rising closer to the surface, altering his consciousness enough that he was willing to challenge who he thought he was. Then he had to trust that who he might become was worth discovering. Once he felt his inner worth, he was free to be curious about flying. And he was free to let his imagination connect him with the idea that he could actually fly even though he didn't know the first thing about it.

As the eagle thinks from this new perspective, as he imagines himself flying, he's not weighed down by the fears of the chickens who are telling him he has no business in the air, that he might crash. He can make his first tentative effort at taking off. This is where tenacity becomes critical. Remember, he thinks he's a chicken. To sustain the power of his inner worth and his trust, curiosity, and imagination, he has to talk to himself continually about the possibility that he might not be a chicken after all. And as his short, shaky flights get longer and smoother, he'll become more confident. Little successes grow into larger ones. Soon, his self-talk will be all about the life of an eagle.

SUMMARY

We become who we say we are, and we say this is who we are because those around us assure us it is so. So, like the eagle, we come to believe we're someone other than who we are. Our saying and being become one. The only way we can truly change and be creatively transformed is by changing our saying, believing, valuing, imagining, and doing. To the degree the eagle says to himself, "I could never fly like that; I'm a chicken not an eagle" or "I would be a fool to try something like that," he will never fly very high.

Insight Questions

Personal Growth

How do you pay attention to your self-talk?

When you talk to yourself, does it tend to be more positive or negative?

Relationships

Do you talk to yourself about what you think others are thinking or feeling when you are with them?

Would you consider yourself more of an optimist or a pessimist when you reflect on your self-talk?

Organizations

What is your self-talk regarding your workplace and your colleagues?

Do your self-talk and what you say to others match?

Part 2

*Flight
Plan*

Innovative InterChange Conditions

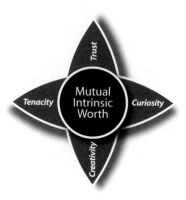

In Part 1, we explored the conditions of worth, trust, curiosity, connectivity, and tenacity; and we talked about how we must align our self-talk with what will free us to become our original self. All of this lays the foundation for Innovative InterChange, the process we'll discuss in Part 2.

Innovative InterChange is a process in which human beings are working together at their best. It's a process in which we must engage in order to be and become our original self. It comprises four phases: Authentic Interacting, Appreciative Understanding, Creative Integrating, and Continual Transforming. When you choose to communicate and transform using Innovative InterChange, you start with the idea that all people have equal intrinsic worth. From that belief, you can say what you mean; you listen to and value diverse perspectives; you're eager to imagine creative ways to solve problems; and you're willing to put in the effort to make this way of communicating a habit.

Chapter 8
Authentic Interacting: Being Your Original Self
(Communication)

It had been one of those hectic days — one of those days when all I wanted to do was kick off my shoes and settle into a nice relaxing meal with the family. And wouldn't you know it, just as I sat down to eat, the phone rang. Without checking caller ID, I answered it. The voice on the other end said, "Hello. Is this Charles?" Before I could reply, the caller continued. "How are you this evening, Charles?" The only person who ever called me Charles was my mother, and she usually called me that when I was in trouble. So I knew in an instant I was talking to a telemarketer.

"What are you selling tonight?" I asked?

"I don't want to sell you anything," he said. "I just want to give you some information."

"Can you honestly say you're not out to sell me anything?" I replied.

The telemarketer then began a scripted speech, and though I kept saying, "I'm not buying," he kept selling.

I was frustrated and fascinated by his tenacity. Someone had coached him to keep talking, regardless of what I said. Problem was, he wasn't interested in what I needed or wanted, and he wasn't being honest about the purpose of his call. We weren't two human beings communicating; we were two roles colliding: Determined seller vs. buyer who's not buying.

Finally, feeling the hungry stares from the dinner table, I decided to bring it to a close.

"I'm still not buying anything, and I'm going to hang up now," I said.

Of course, he kept talking. And true to my word, I hung up. Later, I wondered if there was a guy out there somewhere still talking in a vain effort "not" to sell me something.

How many of us have been that telemarketer at some point in our lives, talking right past someone else because we've got an agenda? We think we're communicating simply because we're talking. The truth is, real communication — Authentic Interacting — is much more complex than that. It takes people who respect and trust each other before they even open their mouths. And when they do start talking, they must do so as their original selves, and the interchange must be free from hypocrisy, deception, and manipulation. Authentic Interacting, the first phase of Innovative InterChange, is sharing the best you know with integrity and listening to the best someone else knows, without being tied to conventional cultural expectations. And it's anything but simple.

Communication process

The communication cycle begins when one person intends to give information to one or more people. The verb "to intend" comes from the Latin word *intendere: in,* meaning "toward," and *tendere,* meaning "to stretch or extend." Quite literally, a person has in mind something she would like to "stretch toward" someone else. Next, it starts to get complex. Many people assume that if they're the ones doing the talking, their responsibility ends once they've expressed whatever they intended to express — it's up to the listener to get the point. But the odds that the listener actually will get the point aren't nearly as great as we might assume. To communicate with each other successfully, the presenter and the listener must make every effort to stay aware of every aspect of the process. The process has six elements:

1. **Communicators:** A sender who formulates and transmits a message and a receiver who receives that message.

2. **Message:** A message comprises ideas, beliefs, values, meanings, and images that a sender intends to share with a receiver.

3. **Channel:** A channel is a method of transmission. It could be face-to-face talking, writing a note, sending an e-mail, making a phone call, sending a text message, etc.

4. **Noise:** Distractions are inevitable. Good communicators are aware of the noise they and their receivers are generating and experiencing and do their best to reduce it to a minimum.

5. **Context:** Context is the setting in which the communication takes place. The setting creates expectations for appropriate communication that are generated by our culture, the physical aspects that surround the interaction, the interacting partners' psychological and emotional states, and social rules.

6. **Feedback:** Both the receiver and the sender provide feedback, or signals, during communication. Feedback can be verbal, meaning actual words, and it can be vocal, meaning sounds that aren't words, such as throat clearing or a change in voice volume or pitch. Feedback can also be non-vocal, such as facial expressions, gestures, and other visible indicators. All of these signals provide the sender and receiver with information about how the other is

reacting to the messages and signals being sent. Feedback is vital in the communication cycle. It allows further interaction to achieve mutual understanding.

A case study

Let's see how easy it is for the complex communication process to break down: A workshop participant — we'll call him Fred — once told me about the time he misunderstood his manager — let's call her Sally — and ended up costing his bank considerable time and money. Fred was preparing to send letters to 5,000 customers announcing a sales promotion. When Sally told Fred not to send the letters because of some last-minute changes in the promotion, Fred didn't hear the word "not," and the mailing went out. What a difference a word makes. The bank had to send another 5,000 letters, correcting the previous letters and apologizing for the error and inconvenience — all of which affected the bank's credibility.

We often assume that we present and listen more effectively than we actually do. So let's take a closer look at Sally and Fred's communication: First, Sally intends to tell Fred not to send the mailing, and she assumes Fred is interested in what she has to say. Second, she must choose the best channel for delivering her message. Is it best to say it face to face? Should she send a memo, an e-mail, or an instant message? Should she call him? It's important to Sally that she is clear, so it's crucial that she present the message in a way that will work for Fred. The presentation will involve much more than her words — it will include the volume and pitch of her voice, the number and length of pauses, and such visual signals as her gestures, facial expressions, and posture.

These physical components are usually more important than the verbal ones; some studies suggest that as little as 7 percent of our message comes through our words, while as much as 60 percent comes through visual signals. In other words, what's coming out of our mouths may not have nearly as much to do with the perception that our behavior creates as we're talking.

A big key to communicating successfully is to express information in a way that takes the listener's frame of reference into consideration. An example: In the late 1960s and early 1970s, I worked on a project to prevent at-risk adolescents from dropping out of school. When I hung out with the kids, I wore jeans, T-shirts, and sneakers, and my vocabulary was fairly colorful. I dressed up my wardrobe and my vocabulary when I called on bank presidents to raise money for the project. Can you imagine what would have happened if I'd walked into the bank using street language or, worse yet, if I had showed up on the streets wearing a suit and wing-tipped shoes, talking like a big-shot corporate guy?

Sally finally decides the best way to deliver her message to Fred is face to face; she thinks that if Fred can see and hear her, there will be little room for him to misunderstand. Fred's role is to translate the message. He takes in, thinks about, and interprets the information he's receiving, filtering it through his existing knowledge, beliefs, values, and perspective. This all happens in seconds and is prone to error — which is why he misses the word "not" and reacts to what he assumes is a valid interpretation, sending out 5,000 letters he wasn't asked to send.

It's hard to be humble

How much responsibility does Sally bear for the misunderstanding? What about Fred? He may be more culpable here — he's the one who doesn't hear the word "not," which brings us to a deeper point about Authentic Interacting: Intentions and choosing the appropriate channel are only the beginning. Authentic Interacting is about ensuring that a presenter's intention and a listener's interpretation match.

Too often, we assume our interpretation is accurate, and we don't feel obligated to verify it. This is where humility becomes crucial. It takes humility and courage to realize that we can make inaccurate interpretations and to admit when we don't know something or that we've made a mistake. Humility and integrity are inseparable. Integrity is presenting the best you know and believe; humility is your willingness to acknowledge there is more to learn. Some people are willing to have integrity when they talk about what they believe but are reluctant to have the same integrity when it comes to what they don't know or understand.

Integrity and humility are born from a sense of one's intrinsic worth. If you think you need someone's approval in order to have worth, you're more inclined to hide things to avoid rejection. In such cases, you compromise your integrity because you prefer acceptance to truth.

Authentic Interacting requires us to be as clear as possible about the knowledge, values, beliefs, meaning, and perspective we want to communicate. As presenters, we must communicate the intent and content of our message so listeners will understand it the way we do. As listeners, we must seek to understand the presenter's intent and content as they understand it and not the way we interpret it. We'll be less apt to miss the "not" in the manager's message if we are humble enough to accept that we might not always understand as well as we think we do.

SUMMARY

The first phase of Innovative InterChange is Authentic Interacting. We tap into it by sharing the best we know with each other and by being humble enough to seek to understand the best others know. Unlike surface-level communication, which often happens between our personas, Authentic Interacting happens when we honor our worth and the worth of the person with whom we're talking.

If we want to experience the satisfaction of being and becoming our original self, we must have the respect, trust, integrity, and humility to authentically interact with others. This is the beginning of our journey and the first flight requirement for the journey toward our original self.

Insight Questions

Personal Growth

Do you feel you're authentic in most of your communication?

Is there any situation in which being inauthentic is a good idea?

Relationships

Do you think most people interact with integrity?

Reflect on whether you listen to others with humility and curiosity.

Organizations

What does your organization do to ensure accuracy of communication among colleagues?

Can businesses afford to be authentic in all their communication?

Chapter 9
Appreciative Understanding: Valuing Your Original Self
(Appreciation)

With tears streaming down his face, a farmer came to a very wise man.

"Oh master, master," he said, "Such ill fortune has befallen me. The pasture gate was left open, and my prize stallion has run away, leaving me with no way to plow my fields and plant my crop. What should I do?"

The wise man sat in silence for some time and then asked, "Is that good, or is that bad?"

The farmer was dumbstruck. What kind of response was that? What insensitivity to a pending disaster! And he went off with great sadness.

Several weeks later, the farmer returned to the wise man with great jubilation and excitement.

"Oh master, master, such wonderful fortune has befallen me. My prize stallion has returned and brought two wild mares with him. I now have three horses to help plow the fields."

The wise man was silent for some time, and then, to the farmer's surprise, he asked again, "Is that good, or is that bad?"

The farmer went off questioning his teacher's wisdom, but he was happy with his state of affairs.

Several weeks later, he returned, again in tears.

"Oh master, master, such ill fortune has befallen me. My son attempted to ride one of the wild mares and was thrown off and broke his back. He cannot help plant crops and plow the fields. I will not be able to harvest. What can I do?"

Predictably, the wise man remained silent for some time and then once again asked, "Is that good, or is that bad?"

The farmer went off in despair. How could such an insensitive person ever have gained a reputation for being wise?

A month later, the farmer returned in great jubilation.

"Oh master, master, fortune has smiled on me. The army came through looking for all the young men to take them off to war. They could not take my son because his back has not healed from the fall."

The wise man was silent again for some time, and then he asked one more time, "Is that good, or is that bad?"

The farmer lives in an "either/or" world. When the world meets his demands and expectations, he's elated. When the world contradicts his demands and expectations, he despairs. He didn't appreciate that the loss of his horse would gain him two more and that this gain would be his son's loss. He has been programmed to agree or disagree with circumstances. The wise man has a different perspective. He understands that all circumstances have "both/and" potential.

"Both/and" thinking is at the core of the second phase of Innovative InterChange: Appreciative Understanding. We can authentically interact all we want, but if our understanding of another person's message doesn't become Appreciative Understanding, the process stalls. Reaching this level of interaction is not easy, of course. We, like the farmer, are programmed to consider people and circumstances as good or bad, right or wrong, smart or dumb, and so on. By the same token, we think of ourselves and others as chickens or eagles, a bird of the ground or a bird of the air, but not both. We have a hard time holding certain perceived differences in our minds at the same time. Most of us have a low tolerance for ambiguity. We allow ourselves to be confused by it, rather than letting it evoke our curiosity.

Embracing contradiction

When we listen to others, we tend to listen in terms of if we agree or disagree with what they're saying. This undermines our ability to perceive the whole picture. Once we hear something we disagree with, we stop really listening. Instead, we start analyzing what's wrong with what we're hearing and begin to plan what to say to bring the other person's thinking in line with our own or at least to make the case for why it's inaccurate.

We migrate toward the people, ideas, situations, and circumstances that agree with our own. It seldom occurs to us that just because we agree with something, that doesn't make it true. Conversely, our disagreement doesn't make something false. Our need to be right doesn't guarantee rightness. Those out of touch with their intrinsic worth often feel threatened when people disagree with them. When a chicken sees an eagle flying high, it doesn't make sense at first glance. It challenges what the chicken knows and expects. It's hard for chickens to appreciatively understand why a creature that appears to be one of them would want to engage in such seemingly foreign behavior. They assume that if their brother isn't content to do what they do, there must be something wrong with him. He's not being himself. Or is he?

As you start the journey to uncover your original self, some people will tell you that you're not being yourself. Like our eagle's chicken friends, they will wonder at the changes you're undergoing. They might decide your urge is dumb, crazy, inappropriate, or, at best, misinformed, and they might tell you they're simply concerned for your well-being. Remember: They're providing advice based on their limited understanding of your new urge to fly high. From their point of view, such an urge is dangerous, and they assume they know all they need to know about your intentions and capabilities. They're not taking the time to be curious about your point of view, which could lead them to appreciatively understand it.

We tend to perceive what we value. We see our preferences and expectations. In order to become our original self, we must challenge our conventional thinking. The real challenge of Appreciative Understanding is realizing that being a good chicken and having eagle urges don't have to be contradictory. The farmer doesn't get this, doesn't understand how to live with ambivalence. Likewise, what seems to be beyond most of our eagle's neighbors is that learning to fly may open myriad opportunities for the rest of them. The eagle won't get much encouragement until his neighbors appreciate his urge to be different. What both the eagle and his neighbors must be open to is discovering that there are benefits and drawbacks to learning to fly in a new way. To ask whether the urge is good or bad is not a useful way to frame the question because it allows only two options. That is precisely what the wise man knows and the farmer doesn't understand.

Power in numbers

Appreciative Understanding isn't only about embracing perceived contradiction; it's about believing that two perspectives can be better than one. When we discover and find value in the similarities and differences between our ideas and beliefs and those of someone else, we can think beyond where we're at any given moment. The similarities affirm our current understanding, while the differences challenge us to look beyond the present to new and different options. This allows us to appreciate the idea of becoming our original self while still seeing value in the person we're being groomed to be by our parents, teachers, peers, and other important people in our lives.

When I was eight years old, my parents decided I should learn to play a musical instrument. My father liked the accordion, so that was the instrument I was given. I had no interest in or appreciation for it at first, but I dutifully practiced. I got to like it, and I got good at it — good enough to play professionally years later. I'd found a way to open my mind to the experience, and it paid off.

This willingness to think outside my limited box served me well as a teenager, too. When I was 15, I fell in love with a girl from the other side of the tracks, as they say. She was from what my family called "culture." We were blue-collar. I listened to Bing Crosby and Johnny Ray, and her parents had groomed her in classical music. I soon discovered that if I wanted to spend Saturday afternoons with her, it wouldn't be at the movies, but at the concert hall. What a drag. How could anyone waste his time listening to symphonies and virtuosos playing dreary, boring music? If you could call it music.

But I went anyway.

And I was bored out of my mind — at first.

Gradually, I began to listen and observe. I heard new combinations of sound, rhythm, and instruments. I heard melodies and counter melodies. The orchestra musicians had dexterity like I had never seen before. The world of classical music was richer and deeper than I'd ever imagined. My horizons were expanding. I was becoming a different person. I realized that you can like Fats Domino and Caruso, Glenn Miller and the Chicago Symphony.

Point is, I am who I am today, in part, because of my first love. After Authentic Interaction with classical music, I gained an Appreciative Understanding of its value. I had, without knowing it, experienced Innovative InterChange. I learned that daring to embrace what you first judge to be negative can result in deepening your capacity for appreciation.

Now keep in mind that appreciating another's point of view doesn't mean you have to like it or agree with it; you simply allow room for it to exist and have merit. So it's okay to question something or someone as long as you're willing to engage in Innovative InterChange with them to discover what commentator Paul Harvey used to call "the rest of the story." We can find value where we initially don't see it or have any inclination to find it. Appreciation is a choice.

SUMMARY

The second phase of Innovative InterChange is Appreciative Understanding, where we understand and acknowledge the value in the unique perspectives of other people.

Appreciative Understanding is rooted in the primary condition of intrinsic worth. When we fail to accept that others have equal worth, it's hard to find value in their thinking and ideas, especially when they differ from our own. When we encounter differences in others, we need to let go of our tendency to judge and criticize and put forth the effort to find value. Appreciative Understanding is about learning to see that the same thing can be positive from one point of view and negative from another and that both can be partially correct and partially in error. When we learn this, we create a positive environment for more Authentic Interacting.

Insight Questions

Personal Growth

In what ways do you think you're an either/or thinker?

What do you do when you disagree with someone?

Relationships

How do you think conversations would be different if people were willing to seek Appreciative Understanding?

What makes it so difficult for some people to understand others? What about you? What makes it hard for you to make the effort to understand others?

Organizations

Many organizations end up with what some call an "argument culture" because of all the disagreeing, debating, and arguing. What is your workplace like?

What do you think makes people compete with others with whom they need to be cooperative?

Chapter 10
Creative Integrating: Becoming Your Original Self
(Integration)

Carole, the marketing director at a global technology company, was concerned as she called her team together for a high-priority strategy meeting. With sales lagging, market share shrinking, and top management pressing the panic button, she knew her team's performance and her managerial skills were under scrutiny. Laying out the numbers, she emphasized that improved performance was a given and that failure wasn't an option. Jobs, including hers, were on the line.

Carole's anxiety was contagious. Everyone in the room had survived the first round of staff cuts, but there was no more fat in the budget to trim. She thought about how it would probably take imagination, innovation, creativity, even playfulness to boost performance. Wait, playfulness? Who was she kidding? It was bite-the-bullet time if they were going to dodge it. So, Carole outlined what seemed like a straight-forward strategy: Define the problem, generate solutions, and develop a plan for implementation.

But the team couldn't even get past "Define the problem," because no two people defined it the same way. Each was caught up in defending his or her own perception of the problem instead of imagining ways to find multiple definitions and, thus, a more comprehensive understanding.

If they were going to turn the company around, the team members needed to break free of their personal need to be right so the group could be successful. As the leader, Carole needed to create a safe environment by giving them permission to question the status quo and by urging them to travel into unfamiliar territory.

Considering a variety of possible solutions takes curiosity, imagination, risk, and trust; simple reason isn't enough. Carole didn't know how to model this for her group, and it's not surprising. While we're still kids, the world drives out much of our creativity, curiosity, and willingness to risk and replaces them with conformity, caution, and reason. But as Einstein said, "Imagination is more important than reason."

Through imagination, we can engage in Creative Integrating, the third phase of Innovative InterChange, in which we have the freedom and capacity to absorb the differences we find among diverse perspectives and use our childlike imaginations to discover new possibilities. Creative Integrating allows us to blend perspectives; make richer, more novel connections; and discover options we might never have found otherwise.

Clearing the air

What might Carole do to move her team members beyond the boundaries of their own frames of reference? First, she needs to focus the team on formulating the problems and not on imagining worst-case scenarios. What is the problem? Is it really several problems? What are other ways of thinking about the problem? Are there other ways to state it? Are we looking at symptoms? What are the systemic issues? Is there something that's been bugging folks for a long time about how this company works or what we assume? What's at the root of that? Is there some way our product or service has changed or failed to change because of wrong assumptions? Instead of thinking about what our competition is doing, is there something we know we can do better than anyone else? Are we still doing things we know we're not all that good at doing?

By giving her team the opportunity to express alternative ideas, perspectives, beliefs, and values, she would allow them to see new possibilities and make new connections. Imagine how this approach might transform your work environment. When people let their minds go and aren't afraid of new ideas, even if those ideas seem counter to their own, they're bound to discover more innovative solutions.

Learning to play again

As did all of the conditions and phases of Innovative InterChange, Creative Integrating came naturally to us as children because we weren't afraid of our imagination. Imagination is the key to Creative Integrating because it allows us to make absurd connections — links between things that from a so-called rational, adult perspective have no apparent similarities. Unfortunately, many adults have forgotten how to play and how to be spontaneous. We often use our imagination to conjure up all kinds of worst-case scenarios. Carole, for example, imagines having to lay off colleagues or losing her own job instead of imagining the team finding creative and innovative solutions.

As a child, you played much of the time. You played superhero, warrior, dinosaur, horse — anything that allowed you to try on different identities. You weren't self-conscious or ashamed. You were liberated. As adults, we're afraid of looking silly, of not being taken seriously by other adults. Parents, teachers, siblings, and friends model and reinforce certain qualities we learn to imitate and develop. Such reinforcement then conditions us to think and behave in certain ways and can limit our ability to explore beyond the definitions we've created for ourselves.

This isn't to say that the personality we've developed as adults isn't valid or vital. This personality is a stabilizing force in our lives. But it's a conditioned, created self, and it's only one version of who we're capable of becoming. By tapping into our imagination, we can mix fact, fantasy, dreams, and memories to create alternative versions of our self.

A defining characteristic

When children use their imagination, they're looking for meaning in the world and in their lives by making connections. They're also exercising their ability to control what they think, believe, and value. Exercising their free will, they often clash with their parents and other authority figures, who don't see the excitement and wonder in exploration and experimentation. Adults often focus on the dangers and potential negative consequences of children's actions, while children focus on the journey and what they might discover along the way.

In his research on how humans think, University of Maryland professor Dr. Mark Turner concludes that imagination is a cognitive ability that truly separates humans from every other species on the planet. He describes imagination as an ability to blend what is with what isn't. For example, we can envision a mouse that talks, a train that flies, or a wardrobe that leads to another world. We have no current evidence to suggest that a chimpanzee, for example, sits around making such "absurd" connections, according to Turner.

In the context of Innovative InterChange, our imagination can connect what is with what is conceivable. We know that in all probability, we're not likely to step through a wardrobe into a strange new world. Yet, such images can become metaphors that lead us to new ways of looking at an issue we're trying to resolve. The company trying to invent a better mousetrap, for example, might brainstorm on the image of the magical wardrobe and decide to establish a process for employees to submit new ideas. The process wouldn't put limitations or pass judgment on the ideas; rather, people would be encouraged to step into the process and let their imaginations run wild. They could come out on the other side with real solutions that might improve a product, the work environment, and the company as a whole.

Turner also says that imagination is what allows us to put ourselves in another person's shoes. It's why we can say such simple things as, "If I were George, I'd buy the mini-van." Indeed, it will expand our frame of mind and open us up to other perspectives. When we're open to different points of view, we're more likely to connect ideas and find new, more creative options that work for everyone.

Conquering your fear

Sadly, many people fear where their imaginations and other people's ideas might take them. They're afraid they'll be forced out of their comfort zones. New ideas do require us to let go of our familiar reality and step into an uncertain future reality. How do you know the new space will be better? How do you know it won't be worse? You don't — not for sure.

I do know from long experience that if we embrace equal worth, trust, curiosity, and connectivity, and if we commit to Authentic Interacting, Appreciative Understanding, and Creative Integrating, we can experience transforming expansion and satisfaction.

This is what we're designed to experience, not just once or twice, but continually. Just as we learn what a banana tastes like by putting it into our mouth, just as we learn to be a manager by managing, to be a writer by writing, so we will experience the transformation of our current perspective by engaging in something new.

So strap on your wings of imagination. Go soar beyond the backyard limitations of your current self. Don't be bashful. Your original self appears strange until you embrace it. And when you do, you experience profound peace and exhilaration, a thrill and freedom that your backyard comfort zone can never rival. Take a risk, make a choice, and start the journey to what you want to become.

SUMMARY

The third phase of Innovative InterChange is Creative Integrating. This is where we use our innate curiosity and imagination to summon our original self and blend it with our current self, which leads to new possibilities for being and becoming. Often, the opportunity for Creative Integrating comes when we're at a crossroads, when we have important decisions to make, when we need to brainstorm. Whether you see such an opportunity as a blessing or a curse is up to you. Are you committed to preserving your current way of being — your comfort zone — and remaining open to becoming more in your creative zone? That is the question.

Insight Questions

Personal Growth

In what ways do you consider yourself to be imaginative?

Why do you think Einstein thought imagination is more important than reason?

Relationships

In conversations with others, you can express your opinion without being influenced by the thinking of others. Reflect on when you approach others with the intent to both understand and learn from them and when you don't.

What do you imagine others will think if you become more of your original self and you care less about convention and others' expectations?

Organizations

Name some ways in which your organization has encouraged its people to think outside of the box.

Some organizations don't want to encourage too much creativity in the workplace. They think it will do more harm than good. What is this struggle about?

Chapter 11
Continual Transforming: Making a Habit of Being and Becoming
(Transformation)

It had been a great year for Bernard, president of a fast-growing accounting firm. The company had exceeded its billing goals, and the client base had doubled. Unfortunately, the other thing that had doubled was Bernard's waistline. Who has time to hit the gym with cocktail parties and hors d'oeuvres every week, not to mention M&Ms around every corner at the office?

But the new year was approaching, and after the last client holiday party, Bernard wanted to start his new diet and exercise regimen, guaranteed to offset the gluttony of the previous year. Of course, he'd had similar aspirations before, but this time he was reading a new fitness book. This time he would succeed. This time he would not give up until his weight was under control — his control. The first few days of the new year were a piece of cake, so to speak. Bernard's enthusiasm was more than enough to get him to the gym by 5:30 every morning, and his will to avoid the candy dish was strong. He was even eating grapefruit and whole wheat toast for breakfast.

But Bernard's good intentions didn't last. He started sleeping in on Mondays, then Tuesdays, then Wednesdays "just this once." He left the healthy breakfast he packed at home a couple times, and he grabbed a few handfuls of chocolate at work to tide him over. Within a month, he was back to his old, comfortable habits, and by year's end, he'd lost the battle of the bulge — again.

It was relatively easy for Bernard to come up with his resolution, but he couldn't translate his intention into a lasting habit. Turning words into deeds and ideas into action takes commitment, tenacity, practice, and feedback. It's more than, "I'd like to do something" or "I intend to do something." It takes a daily, hourly act of will. Bernard imagined himself slim; he intended to become that way, but old habits foiled his imagination and intentions.

Habits are the stuff perspectives are made of. Habits form the edges of our comfort zone and the boundaries of our frame of reference. They're critical to our stability and identity. They define us. Nevertheless, they become a problem when they confine us. They keep us from being authentic with others and with ourselves, being open to things we dislike, and using our imaginations. We're in the habit of protecting ourselves from transformation because transformation is uncharted territory, and we like to stay where it's familiar and requires less effort. The fourth phase of Innovative InterChange is Continual Transforming, using the Innovative InterChange skills and tools to develop new habits that will lead us to new ways of being, working, and living.

Anatomy of a habit

Confucius said, "What I hear I forget, what I see I remember, and what I do I understand." Yet, we often do things without really changing. It's only when something becomes a habit that it becomes a part of us. Habit formation starts with intention to change and a vision of what success will look like. Once we've seen the eagle soaring in the sky, we have a picture of that success. Next, we have to start practicing. Concentration and repetition are the only ways practice is going to pay off — they're especially crucial when we're first starting out and we're stumbling. Eventually, the new skill or new thinking will become as unconscious as other habits we've mastered; we just have to be willing to put up with looking incompetent in the meantime.

How long until we're competent? Remember, it typically takes thirty to ninety days for an adult to develop new thinking and behavioral habits. The length of time varies with the level of motivation, current skill and knowledge level, opportunities to practice, the complexity of the habit to be mastered, and the degree to which the new behavior opposes existing habits. Habituation is less a matter of what to think than how to think.

It's a great idea to fly like an eagle. But merely being drawn to the sky, feeling the urge to fly, and even making the decision to fly don't teach you the mechanics of flight and the necessary navigational skills. The urge to become our original self doesn't tell us how to do it. While some of our habits are certainly genetic, many are conditioned early on and become part of our hard-wiring. If we want to develop new habits, it helps to understand that hard-wiring process. There are four primary motivators — call them the "critical Cs" — in new habit formation: celebration, correction, confrontation, and consequences.

As children, we were rewarded when we did something that pleased our parents — we got to celebrate, the first C. The celebration brought us pleasure and reinforced our habit formation. This is why you hear behavioral and management experts say, "You tend to get the behavior you reward." Positive reinforcement, tied as closely as possible to the desired behavior, is a major key to developing a habit.

Because learning anything new is awkward at first, you're bound to have to stop, correct your mistakes, and start over. The most effective kind of correction, the second C, is that which doesn't dwell on faults but coaches us on how to fix them. Until we catch our errors on our own, it's helpful to ask for help. And it's always easier to accept mistakes if we're doing so in the midst of celebrating what we've done right.

The third C is confrontation. When celebration and correction fail to cement a new habit, we often give up. Confronting ourselves when we've slacked off is not as much fun as celebration, but it can remind us of our commitment to learn and form a habit and get us back on track.

Sometimes, even confrontation isn't enough to shake us loose from old patterns. In that case, we may have to accept the fourth C, consequences. At work, they might be as mild as a reprimand or as serious as getting fired. In our personal lives, it might be the disappointment of gaining back the ten pounds or a more serious medical scare. Consequences need not deflate you but can serve to remind you why you decided to pursue the new habit in the first place. Perhaps the worst consequence isn't the reprimand or punishment; it's that by avoiding or delaying change, you're missing out on the transformation to your original self.

All of these motivators make up the feedback we get as we're developing the new habit. Without feedback, it's impossible to know if we're making progress. We need to know when we're getting it right, when we need to make an adjustment, and when we're completely missing the mark.

Surviving the setbacks

The tricky thing about change is that we won't have all the information up front. We have no idea how hard or easy it's going to be. The decision to stop smoking, for example, doesn't take into account how intense our nicotine cravings will be or all of the people who will offer us a cigarette just when we'd love to have one. In order to form new habits, we must have a strong belief in the value of the new way of thinking and behaving.

When we value the goal, we're motivated to achieve it. We've got to have a plan for what to do when the temptation to revert to the old habit, like smoking, is strong. Will we walk away, chew some gum, or be reminded to stick to our goal by a token of some kind in our pocket? For Bernard, perhaps a picture of his twenty-something slimmer self posted on the fridge is the motivation he needs to step away from the donut.

Distractions, temptations, and lack of feedback aren't the only things that get in the way of developing and sticking to new habits. Human beings often resist even starting anything new if it runs the risk of failure. We're in the habit of needing to look good, to be in control, and to appear as if we've got it all together. Such fear-driven habits may reduce our exposure to mistakes and failure, but when we shy away from opportunities to learn, grow, and be changed, we lose out on the chance to experience the satisfaction of creative transformation.

Whatever the new habit, chances are, we won't be very good at it right away. So we have to let go of the fear of looking silly or incompetent if we're going to survive the early stages, when we're most prone to giving up. During this stage, not only do we have our own fears to contend with; we have the skepticism and cynicism of those around us to keep at bay. It's a lot to manage, but again, if you're willing to pay the price, you can keep the change.

SUMMARY

Authentic Interacting can provide us with new information, meaning, and ways of thinking. When we appreciatively understand the information and discover its value for us, we can look for ways to make the information and the different perspectives a part of us. Yet, it isn't until we reach the Continual Transforming phase that we can make a habit of living from a new perspective. Only then can we experience the transformational change in our lives that comes from being our original self.

When we make Innovative InterChange a way of life, we can consistently experience our original self and the satisfaction that accompanies such transformation and growth. By challenging the inertia of our existing habits, we establish new ones. When Innovative InterChange becomes a habit, we can be and do our best while continuing to actualize more of our potential.

Insight Questions

Personal Growth

Think back to the New Year's resolutions you failed to keep. Then think of those you kept. What made the difference?

If you really wanted to form a new habit, what in you would typically resist? Why?

Relationships

Why do some people find it hard to support others who are trying to develop new habits?

How have people reacted to you when you've tried to form new habits?

Organizations

Have you ever worked in an organization that had a "flavor of the week" attitude when it came to making changes? What caused such an attitude? How did employees respond to it?

What is the most important thing an organization can do in order to encourage new ways of thinking and behaving?

Chapter 12
Innovative InterChange:
A Two-Fold Flight Plan

You're watching a typical Sunday morning political talk show. Two senators, one liberal and one conservative, have been invited to discuss their opposing views on a major world event. After the host recaps the issue and introduces the guests, he directs the first question to the conservative congresswoman.

The show then heads down a predictable path: As the conservative senator starts to answer, the camera pans over to the liberal senator, his head moving back and forth in apparent disagreement. The more he shakes his head, the more animated the congresswoman becomes.

Finally, the liberal senator can't wait any longer. He plunges into his remarks without even waiting for the conservative senator to finish or for the host to prompt him. He starts speaking in opposition to what he has heard — which is quite different from what the conservative has said or intended to say. He insists that she has not presented the facts and has subverted the truth to spin her case. The conservative senator then counters, saying it's the liberal who is spreading misinformation.

At this point, they're both talking over each other, while each is demanding that the other stop talking and listen. The host finally jumps in to try to bring order and clarification, but no one stops talking, and the din gets even louder.

Little happens these days to make the world of public deliberation — or the world of any deliberation, for that matter — a place where truth seeking is the primary goal. Most of us are more interested in pushing our own views than in listening to another's. Over the last four chapters, we've examined Innovative InterChange, a process rooted in the notion that none of us really knows the total truth, and we're certainly not going to discover it on our own. We can, however, combine the best we do know with the best other people know, in pursuit of a broader understanding of the world and our place in it.

This process of Innovative InterChange will build lasting relationships that encourage individuals and organizations to be and become more fully and profoundly their best and bring us all closer to that deep satisfaction we all seek.

The conditions

This flight toward the original self begins by discovering our intrinsic worth, which is equal for everyone. Yet, while we're all equal in intrinsic worth, none of us is equal in extrinsic worth. We're not all equal in athletic ability, intelligence, aptitude, genetics, and a whole host of other things. The challenge is to learn to distinguish between the two kinds of worth and to rediscover and accept our intrinsic worth. This means the eagle must accept that he's an eagle at heart. He's not crazy for having urges to fly. Likewise, you're not crazy for wanting to experience the satisfaction of being and becoming your original self. In Part 3, we'll explore ways of getting back to our original self, what T. S. Eliot meant when he wrote:

We shall not cease from exploration
And the end of all our exploring
Will be to arrive where we started
And know the place for the first time.
(T.S. Eliot, "Little Gidding")

Innovative InterChange

Combine the sense of our intrinsic worth with the ability to trust ourselves and the assumption that other people have integrity; the curiosity to explore and appreciate new ideas; the ability to use our imagination to connect diverse perspectives to create possibilities; and the tenacity to turn new skills into sustainable habits — and you have the foundation for engaging in Innovative InterChange:

Authentic Interacting

To share the best you know with integrity and to listen with humility to, understand, and learn from the best someone else knows.

When we know our worth, when we trust, and when we act with integrity and humility, we can authentically interact with others. When we engage on this level, our relationships and interactions can have more meaning.

Appreciative Understanding

To resist your culturally programmed tendency to think in "either/ or" terms; to look for the similarities and differences between your perspective and someone else's; and to be willing to understand and acknowledge the context of and value in both points of view.

To truly understand what other people are trying to tell us, we must appreciate the context in which they're sharing information. Our tendency is to bring that information into our own context, which modifies it. Appreciative Understanding means not only understanding the information, knowledge, and actions of others, but also appreciating their frame of reference. This isn't always easy. Following the tragedy of September 11, so many people were asking, "Why do they hate us so much? How could we possibly make sense of such an act of violence, and why would we want to?" Nevertheless, if there is to be any hope for reconciliation in the world, we must make that effort to understand and appreciate the intentions and motives of other people — all people.

Creative Integrating

To absorb the differences you find between your perspective and someone else's and then to use your imagination to discover new possibilities.

When our current way of being, thinking, and behaving has run out of options, it's time to be creative. We need to make new connections and generate alternatives. Creative Integrating helps us do these things — it transforms our perspective and brings us to the heart of where our created self and our original self are entwined.

Continual Transforming

To resist your culturally programmed tendency to become rigid, stubborn, and trapped in the ruts of conventional communication; to have the discipline to practice and develop habits that will lead to new ways of thinking, behaving, and being.

We're not defined and confined by our hardwiring. If we believe we're a certain way and that definition is reinforced over time, we set the stage for a stagnant life. The more entrenched our habits become, the less willing we are to challenge them. When we're open to continual transforming, we reinvent ourselves every day; we develop new habits that transform us into an even richer level of being and becoming.

SUMMARY

Innovative InterChange is a two-fold commitment.

First, we must commit to engaging in the phases: Authentic Interacting, Appreciative Understanding, Creating Integrating, and Continual Transforming. Second, we must learn and consistently use a set of skills and tools that help us translate our intention into action. Once the eagle made up his mind to fly, he had to develop his flying capabilities. He had to master new navigational skills and strengthen his wings. He knew what he needed to do, and then he practiced, practiced, practiced. Now that we know the path to reclaiming our original self, in Part 3 we can learn more about the thinking tools and behavioral skills that will keep us airborne and flying infinitely higher.

Insight Questions

Personal Growth

Think of a time when you listened to someone, understood, found value in what he or she said, and ended up making some of it a part of your life.

What would it take for you to make the journey inward toward your original self? Which part of the journey would be the most difficult for you? Which part would be the simplest?

Relationships

Think about a very close friend. Think about how you interact with that friend. Make a list of some of the things that make the relationship valuable.

Think about someone with whom you have conflict. List some of the things that make the relationship conflicted.

What are the differences in your two lists? Which one most resembles Innovative InterChange? Which one feels the best?

Organizations

What percent of your organization's culture consistently practices the tools and skills of Innovative InterChange? Which behaviors suggest this to you?

In what ways do you think your organization would benefit if it made Innovative InterChange thinking tools and behavioral skills into priorities?

Part 3

*Flight
Preparations*

Innovative InterChange
Conditions & Phases

In Part 2, we analyzed the Innovative InterChange process, a series of natural phases we go through when we're thinking, behaving, and communicating at our best, most productive level. Through Authentic Interacting, Appreciative Understanding, Creative Integrating, and Continual Transforming, we can connect with our original self and with other people in a deeper, more meaningful way. Now it's time to get practical. For Innovative InterChange to work, you must be willing to go beyond conventional thinking and behaving to a place where you can continually transform. To help you find that place, you need eight thinking tools and behavioral skills, which you will discover and practice using in Part 3. These tools — when the conditions of worth, trust, curiosity, connectivity, and tenacity have been established — allow you to engage in Innovative InterChange. They allow you to be an eagle and follow your urge to fly.

Chapter 13
Reclaiming Your Worth

Sally was eight years old, and it was the night of her first piano recital. Her proud parents were all smiles, ready to capture every moment with the new digital camera they purchased for the occasion. Grandpa and Grandma had driven more than 100 miles to be there for the big event.

Sally was number seven on the program. She watched with excitement as the first two performers played their pieces. Then something happened. She began to feel a sinking feeling in the pit of her stomach. Her imagination started conjuring up pictures that sent her heart racing and her palms sweating. What if she made a big mistake? Worse yet, suppose she forgot her music. What if she just sat there with a totally blank mind and had to leave the stage in tears?

One negative thought after another paraded through her head. She was finding it hard to breathe. Her thoughts were suddenly interrupted by the applause for the sixth performer. The enthusiasm and love of her family suddenly faded as she stood and headed for center stage, her worth as a human being riding on the outcome.

Most of us tie our intrinsic worth to our performance and to getting applause, approval, and acceptance from the outside world. We're in the habit of basing our worth on outside judgment of who we are or ought to be and how others feel about what we're doing. We must begin looking inward to discover what approval can never provide. No one can make that journey for us. Rediscovering our intrinsic worth is the starting point of our journey. When we travel through life rooted in our original worth, we see and do things differently than when we are seeking validation from others.

Let's look more intensively at the psychological distinction between self-worth and self-esteem. Remember, *esteem* comes from the Latin word meaning "to estimate" — it's about an external, cultural judgment of what it means to be successful and worthy of praise and acceptance. Self-worth, on the other hand, starts from an internal sense of value; and the confidence, optimism, and self-regard that come from our intrinsic value aren't subject to cultural approval. They are ours to keep.

In his research into what predicts high performance, author and consultant Marcus Buckingham talks about the difference between the popular notion of self-*esteem* and what he calls self-*efficacy*. Drawing conclusions from an American Psychological Society study, he suggests that self-esteem is emotionally based, tied to performance and the judgments of others; whereas self-efficacy is the behavioral manifestation of a person's intrinsic worth.

Buckingham suggests that people with self-efficacy are likely to perform at a higher level than are those with high self-esteem. Self-efficacy is less apt to be complicated by performance anxiety and the need to save face at any cost. There is a profound difference between people who act out of a conditioned need to remain safe and people who act out of an innate urge to become more than they are.

Back where you started

Accepting our intrinsic worth is one of the most critical decisions any of us will ever make. The moment we do, we discover we have an internal compass, a way of orienting ourselves in life. When we use that compass, we can feel when we're aligned with our original self and when we have veered off course. The feelings are subtle. Most of us were more in tune with them when we were young. The next exercise can help you get in touch with some of these feelings.

Reflect on this... Quiet yourself. Breathe deeply. Think back to a time when you were at peace, preferably when you were alone, a time when you felt a deep sense of relaxation, and joy, a time when you had no particular thing to do or place to go. Perhaps you were outside on a warm day, feeling a gentle breeze, gazing at a few white clouds, listening to the birds. Maybe you were on a beach with white-capped waves washing the shoreline and gulls hovering effortlessly in the sky. Perhaps you were most relaxed in a favorite chair, listening to music. Or maybe you liked to sit on the front porch and watch the world go by. Take a moment to find your favorite place.

Now focus on how you're feeling. Capture the sense of oneness with your surroundings, the sense that you're aligned with the world. You experience deep satisfaction, a sense of peace and joy.

Such an experience conveys a sense of unfamiliar familiarity. It's unfamiliar because most of us don't experience it as often as we once did and familiar because it still rings true. It's a sense of being home and belonging. At such a moment, we can experience and accept ourselves simply as we are, no pretense or performance required. We are for an instant fully who we are and free of comparisons, competitors, and criticisms. We're momentarily apart from our everyday world and a part of something far greater than our ordinary experience. At such moments, our created self and our original self are aligned. Neither self is a threat to the other. Such rare moments have the ring of truth, peace, and contentment.

Unlike our original self, our created self is designed to align with an external compass set by the values of our culture. When we perform and achieve according to society's guidelines, we experience temporary pleasure and excitement. These are emotions. They are a reaction to being aligned with what others applaud, approve, and accept. There is nothing wrong with emotions of contentment — it's a problem only when they become a substitute for deeper feelings of peace, joy, and fulfillment. Pleasure and excitement are false fixes and can distract and throw us out of alignment with our internal compass. This distinction between emotions and feelings is extremely fine.

> **Reflect on this...** Think about what happens when you have a nightmare. You wake up abruptly, and you're out of breath. Your heart is pounding, your stomach is tense, your palms are sweaty. You're incredibly anxious. You're anesthetized to the real, but more subtle, feeling of being physically safe in your own bed, in your own house, because your body is reacting with emotions appropriate for the images your mind conjured up in the dream.

Understanding rejection

Just as our imagination can trump tactile feelings, our preoccupation with the expectations and demands of our created self can obstruct the satisfying reality of our original self. Our habitual ways of thinking shape our consciousness. Because we're not in the habit of experiencing our original self, we must make a conscious choice to focus on the feelings that are part of that original self. Try this exercise:

> **Reflect on this...** Think of a time when you were rejected by a significant other — maybe a time when a parent, spouse, sibling, or close friend was genuinely disappointed in you for some reason. Your performance wasn't what you or others expected. What were your emotions? What were you thinking about yourself? How were you feeling about yourself? Were you angry, afraid, hurt, guilty? Make a list of your emotions and behaviors.

Ask yourself what generated the emotions. You don't need to justify why you felt a certain way; just reflect on what brought about the emotions.

Remember that as a young child, you naturally learned from success and failure. Both could teach you something. Each could help you grow and develop. This was true until you started attaching your intrinsic worth to outward success and assumed you could lose your worth if you made mistakes or others were disappointed with your performance.

Does rejection have to be so painful? It's not a crazy question. We've been programmed to believe that rejection is inevitably negative. Not so fast. Why can't we feel good when we make mistakes? Why do we have to be liked by everyone for everything we say and do? Remember, rejection feels bad because an external message that we're unworthy is colliding with the internal message that our worth is rock solid. You're telling yourself you're worthless and worthwhile at the same time, and the tension between the messages is where the pain originates.

Until we appreciatively understand this conflict between our created self and our original self, we will not experience the deep satisfaction of integrating them, and we will continue to feel that pain. This understanding starts when you realize that your worth comes from your uniqueness. You're an unrepeatable event in the cosmos — there never has been, there isn't now, and there never will be another person quite like you. So you don't have to distinguish yourself through competition with others or living up to outside expectations. Such extrinsic pursuits won't make you happier or more satisfied, and they can't define you any more clearly than can the mere fact that you exist and have value because you exist.

Acknowledging the internal, infinite stability of your uniqueness also frees you from the urge to seek satisfaction in external security and control, which are temporary conditions. You're secure until the next stock market slump, the next terrorist attack, the next health problem. Try as you might, you can't control any of it. Your satisfaction must be tied to less tentative things — such as your intrinsic worth. Below is another way to get in touch with it.

> **Try this exercise...** Think about someone you truly respect. Think specifically about what that person says and does. Focus on behavior. What attracts you to this person? What behavior do you respect? Divide a sheet of paper in half, and on the left side, list those behaviors.
>
> Now, think of someone you have trouble respecting, or even dislike. Think specifically about what this person says and does. Focus on the person's behavior. What is it about it that repels you? What behavior don't you respect? On the right side of your paper, list those behaviors.
>
> Study the behaviors on the left side and notice how many of them are positive, or what we can refer to as "worth-based." Study the behaviors on the right side and notice how many are what we can call "hurt-based."
>
> Notice that you, from time to time, express both sets of behaviors. There are times when we act from our worth and times when we act from our hurt. The key is to become aware of when we're acting from our worth-based original self and do all we can to continue doing so. Likewise, when we are acting from our hurt-based created self, we must try to remember our commitment to replacing hurt-based habits with worth-based ones. This takes tenacity and discipline. It forms the basis for our capacity to engage in Innovative InterChange and to experience the satisfaction of life-transforming creativity.

SUMMARY

Reclaiming your worth starts when you reconnect with it. As children, we have a much stronger sense of our worth-based original selves; so reflecting on times when you were younger and felt all was right with the world will help you make that connection. It's also important to remember that anxiety, hostility, guilt, shame, and blame are emotional responses that come when you allow extrinsic judgments to come between you and your original self. You can temporarily mask those emotions, but temporary fixes fail to bring you the deep joy, peace, and satisfaction that come when you're in touch with your intrinsic worth.

Only when we've made a habit of accepting and trusting our unique, original self and the original selves of others will we start moving from the backyard to the cloudless sky.

Insight Questions

Personal Growth

In order to re-experience your intrinsic worth, you must be willing to make it a priority and practice giving it your undivided attention. What are some ways you can ensure that you focus more on becoming your original self?

What will you do to catch yourself acting from your original self? What will you do when you catch yourself acting out of hurt instead of worth?

Relationships

How can you help others become more aware of their original selves?

How can you anticipate and choose your responses when someone rejects you?

Organizations

How can you help your workplace focus on intrinsic worth and not just performance criteria for assessing extrinsic worth?

Chapter 14

Authentic Interacting Tool 1

Intent Sharing

A gem collector decided to specialize in collecting high-quality jade. He wanted only the finest jade available, so he searched for months for a gemologist to teach him how to distinguish the real thing from an impostor.

He finally found one, and they agreed, for a sizable price, to meet once a week for ten weeks.

When the collector arrived for his first lesson, the gemologist gave him a perfect specimen of jade and asked him to observe it for one hour. Full of curiosity and excitement, the collector examined the gem closely from every angle. After the hour was up, he went home, eager to return the following week to learn more. The next week, the gemologist again handed the collector a piece of high-quality jade and left him to study it. While the man was disappointed to be doing the same thing, he followed the instructions. The third week, the lesson was the same. The collector's disappointment turned to irritation. He was paying hard-earned money, and all he had done was sit for three hours staring at pieces of high-quality jade. It seemed like an expensive waste of time.

The following weeks were no different. The collector complained to the gemologist. He complained to his friends and family. He decided he would go to the final session, and if he wasn't satisfied, he would take action to get his money back. Later, when he was *telling his lawyer about the last lesson, he said, "The guy not only gave me another piece of jade to examine; he gave me a poor-quality piece at that!"*

One hopes that the gem collector eventually realized what the master had done for him. One of the best ways to distinguish between the authentic and the phony is to study and Appreciatively Understand what the authentic looks like. How can we distinguish between the two in ourselves? Authentic people say and do what they intend to say and do, even if other people disagree and disapprove. Inauthentic people contradict what they know to be true for themselves because they feel a need to please other people. When there is a disconnect between who we are and who we say and act like we are, it breeds confusion and suspicion, and people will second-guess our motives.

Intent Sharing, the first thinking and behavioral skill we use in the Authentic Interacting phase, is about communicating your intent and your message up front with integrity. Your words aren't saying one thing while your voice and body are saying something else. The listener senses that consistency and assumes you can be trusted and that the communication between you is transparent and open. There's also a greater chance that the listener will interpret your message accurately. As you seek to make your communication more authentic, the following guidelines will help you share your intent more efficiently and effectively.

1. Have mutual respect.

Authentic Interacting is rooted in mutual respect. If you distort the truth or withhold it from someone, you're not respecting that person or yourself. You're not being authentic, and you're dishonoring your intrinsic worth. We make excuses for such deception, such as not wanting to hurt someone's feelings or thinking it's in a person's best interest not to know something. Sometimes, we're inauthentic because we're taking advantage of someone. Authentic Interacting is sharing with integrity the best we know. It demonstrates respect for the presenter's intended message and for the listener's trustworthiness and ability to understand.

2. Clarify your intentions.

It's critical that you be clear about what you intend to communicate to another. As writer Stephen Covey says in *Seven Habits of Highly Effective People*, begin with the end in mind. When we're not clear about what we want to say, the honest thing to do is to let the listener know that we're still trying to figure out our intent even though we've started talking. When we pretend to be more certain than we are, we cause confusion and undermine integrity and respect. The more we're clear about our intentions before we speak, the greater the probability we'll be understood.

3. Consider different perspectives.

Whatever any of us intends to communicate comes from our perspective. If we want to be authentic, we must keep in mind that the listener has a different perspective, and that not all perspectives are equal. What we actually see and hear from each other — if we even see and hear certain things at all — are filtered through our knowledge and experience. It's amazing how many of us forget this. We assume that if something makes sense to us, it makes the same sense to everyone else.

> **Reflect on this...** Imagine yourself in a conversation about the solar system with a seven-year-old. You're attempting to explain how gravity holds the planets in their orbits, when you see the child's eyes glazing over. You realize you're going to have to use different words and images than you might use with an adult because you know a lot more about the solar system than a seven-year-old child does.

Now, focus on how you are feeling about the conversation. You might be frustrated because the child is having a hard time understanding you at the level you intend to communicate. You might be frustrated with yourself for not being able to make it clear. You also might start to develop an appreciation for the difference that experience and education can make in understanding.

Now, imagine you are having the same conversation about the solar system with Einstein. This time, you're like the seven-year-old, and he's the one with greater knowledge and experience.

Focus on your feelings about this conversation. Your frustration may now come from your failure to understand at the level Einstein is intending for you to understand.

Differences do make a difference. We communicate differently when we're the teacher than when we're the student — the hard part is recognizing which one we are at a given moment. Here's another exercise that shows how crucial your experience and perspective are to seeing what's right in front of you.

Try this exercise... Read the following sentence and count how many times the letter f occurs:

FEATURE FILMS ARE THE RE-
SULT OF YEARS OF SCIENTI-
FIC STUDY COMBINED WITH
THE EXPERIENCE OF YEARS.

Most people count five or fewer. The answer is six. Why do most of us fail to see all six the first time? First, some of the f 's appear at the beginning of a word or line. This sets up a visual expectation that all the f 's will be at the beginning of the words and lines, so we miss the f in of, which appears three times in the sentence. Another reason is that usually, we pronounce f with an f sound, not the v sound in of. So, again, we're not looking for it in the word *of*. And a lot of times, readers skip over small words like *of* completely.

See how easy it is to miss things because of perception? Now, your perception may have been more limited than that of someone who saw all six *f* 's. It's not unusual for there to be a discrepancy in our extrinsic worth, which is where our knowledge and comprehension lie. The important thing to remember and appreciate is that this discrepancy doesn't exist at the level of our intrinsic worth. We're all equal at that level. It's when we forget that, when we have a low sense of intrinsic worth, that we feel threatened and get defensive when our perspective is challenged. We can become blind to the value in the perspectives of others, as we became blind to the *f*'s in the exercise above. People from all along the spectrum rarely feel confident enough to explore the differences in their frames of reference to see what they can learn from each other; opposing ideals simply become fodder for argument and further division.

So, how do we master the skill of thinking from the listener's perspective? How do we learn to anticipate how someone will hear and react to our message so that we can express it appropriately? It takes commitment, concentration, and practice. It's also helpful to understand the different styles people use to communicate, think, and relate. There are many instruments on the market that can help with this. Most of these instruments — such as the Myers-Briggs, Social Styles, Communication Style Survey, Herrmann Brain Dominance, and DISC — not only categorize people's styles, they help us appreciate how those styles can be strengths and weaknesses.

In addition to considering how our communication style may differ from our listener's style, it's useful to keep in mind linguistic differences. The same words and phrases often mean different things to different people. Such phrases as *global warming* and such words as *liberal* and *conservative* can evoke radically different reactions from those who say them and those who hear them.

4. **Stay humble.**

While it may sound obvious that none of us has the ultimate and final perspective, it's amazing how many of us forget that all perspectives are limited, including our own. Of greater concern is when we see all the right things about our own perspective and find it quite easy to point out all the flaws we perceive in other people's perspectives. Presenters can increase authenticity, mutual respect, and trust by acknowledging that their views are limited, partial, and susceptible to error, and by welcoming input from others.

When we present an idea as if it can't be challenged, the listener often becomes defensive and argumentative. When we're open to admitting our limitations, it invites others to respond to what we've said and what they've heard. We can have a more meaningful dialogue when we're humble and let the listener know we're aware of our limitations.

5. **Organize and bite-size.**

The classic style of presentation is this: Tell your listeners what you're going to tell them. Tell them. Then tell them what you told them. Some may think it's an outdated approach, but it's still useful, especially if the listeners are unfamiliar with the subject. Given all the miscommunication and misunderstanding in the world, it's better to irritate listeners and make sure they get what you're saying than to avoid the irritation and run the risk that they misinterpret the message. This method allows you to put your information into logical order and into bite-size pieces, which are easier for people to fully digest.

6. **Pick the right time and place.**

If the message is important, so is its timing. Many of us have fallen into the habit of assuming that if we think something is important enough for us to say, then it's important enough for others to stop what they're doing and listen. That's not necessarily true. You should ask your listener if he or she has the time to stop and listen before you start talking. It's also not true that every place is the best location to have certain conversations, even when others do have the time to listen. Perhaps the subject needs to be discussed in private; maybe the listener needs a quieter room or needs to sit down in order to concentrate on what you're saying. Paying attention to all of these factors can help us be more effective and efficient communicators.

7. **Check for shared meaning.**

Once you've delivered your message, a good last step is to check how successful you were at communicating what you intended to communicate. A simple question such as, "Does that make sense?" can give listeners an opportunity to tell you they're with you or that they need more. Don't assume the listener understood you.

SUMMARY

William Shakespeare's Hamlet said, "This above all: to thine own self be true, and it must follow, as the night the day, thou canst not then be false to any[one]." Authentic Interacting is about having the courage to say and do what you intend to say and do; it's about sharing your intent with integrity. There are six main guidelines for Intent Sharing: 1) have mutual respect; 2) clarify your intentions; 3) consider different perspectives; 4) stay humble; 5) organize and bite-size your message; 6) pick the right time and place; and 7) check for shared meaning.

Intent Sharing isn't without its hazards, though; not everyone will appreciate our integrity, and some may even attempt to take advantage of our humility. We must have the courage to not let these obstacles keep us from moving toward our original self and the satisfaction it brings.

Insight Questions

Personal Growth

How authentic are you in your daily interactions with others?

What is the hardest part about being authentic when you communicate with others?

Relationships

How do you think your family and friends would react to your efforts to be authentic with them? Imagine some specific conversations.

Why do you think so many people confuse humility and humiliation?

Organizations

How does your organization encourage integrity? Humility?

How is the communication in your organization? Effective? Efficient? Innovative?

Chapter 15

Authentic Interacting Tool 2

Confirmed Paraphrasing

Jerry loved football. He loved to settle in on the couch and lose himself in a game. Sara, Jerry's spouse, couldn't care less. And the more time he spent watching football, the more Sara felt stress and strain in their relationship. She longed to have quality time with Jerry, but she felt like she was no match for the TV remote. Even when she could catch him between commercials, cell phone conversations, and buddies dropping by, she found him aloof and indifferent to her interests. He seemed preoccupied with himself. Today was no exception. As he passed through the family room, Sara asked him for some time.

"Jerry!"

"Yeah, what do you want?"

"I need to talk to you about some things that need to be done around here."

"Can't it wait?" Jerry asked.

"I need you to hear me out on this, Jerry," Sara said, hoping he might respond this time.

"I hope it isn't about the kids again," he said.

"As a matter of fact, it is. They miss having time with you. You're gone a lot, and even when you're here, you're not spending time with them — even on Sundays."

"Sundays! Here we go again. The one day I have to kick back and chill out! You want to take that away?"

"I'm not saying you're not—"

"I know what you're saying!" Jerry screamed. "You're telling me I'm not a good father, that I spend more time watching football than I do paying attention to my kids. I don't need this."

"You're not listening!" Sara shouted.

"I've heard everything you said," Jerry replied.

And so it went, until Jerry walked out, slamming the door behind him.

"You're not listening!" How often have you heard someone say that? Spouses have been accusing each other of this for decades — as have parents and children, employers and employees, teachers and students, Democrats and Republicans, and the list goes on.

It's difficult for many people to entertain the thought that they may not be good listeners. When we do challenge our assumptions about how well we listen, we're more open to the number one priority when it comes to listening — seeking first to understand. When you use Confirmed Paraphrasing, the second behavioral tool in the Authentic Interacting phase, you listen with humility to a presenter's message; you restate that message in your own words; and you verify that you understand it the way the presenter intended.

Below are some things you can do to be effective at Confirmed Paraphrasing:

1. **Have mutual respect and stay humble.**

One of the best ways to show respect for someone is to take the time to listen to what he or she has to say. People who keep checking their watches, glancing out a window, or finishing someone else's sentences hardly convey interest, let alone respect. Respect honors another person's intrinsic worth.

Humility is another key to effective listening. The word humility comes from the Latin word for ground or earth. The earth is receptive to many things, including seeds. Likewise, a humble listener is receptive to the seeds of thought from other people, without filtering or prematurely judging the information.

2. **Look closely; listen carefully.**

Appreciative Listeners are good observers. In face-to-face communication, they take in as much visual and auditory information from the presenter as possible. The word *observation* comes from an old Middle English word related to the watch towers on medieval castles and fortresses. Observers in the towers were there to sound signals about anything approaching the tower. In science, a good observer attempts to be objective, protecting the data from undue prejudice and bias. Likewise, a good listener aims to keep the presenter's message uncontaminated by not filtering or prematurely interpreting it.

Try this exercise... To gauge your own ability to observe and be objective, try the following exercise with a partner, or if you're alone, do it while you're watching TV with the sound muted at first. Your objective is to describe the behavior you see and resist the urge to interpret it.

If you're working with a partner, sit facing each other. Ask your partner to talk for one minute about something that interests him or her. You should stay quiet. In fact, you don't even have to try to understand what's being said. Simply observe the person's physical movements. Focus on facial expressions, such as eye and eyebrow movement. Watch for turns of the head, gestures, and if he or she leans forward, backward, or to one side.

Now describe what you saw. For example, you might have

observed that the person raised his or her eyebrows, fidgeted, and made lots of gestures. Just don't interpret what you think the movements meant.

Now sit with your back to your partner. Ask him or her to talk for another minute about something. Concentrate this time on the person's voice — it might help to close your eyes. Listen specifically for changes in volume, pitch, and pace. Are there pauses? Are they long or short, frequent or occasional? Again, simply describe what you hear. Don't interpret what you think it means.

You and your partner should face each other, and your partner should talk one more time about any topic. Watch the body language; listen carefully to the person's voice; and, this time, focus on the words. Still, resist the urge to filter and interpret what's being said. Simply observe the physical and vocal behavior, and listen to the words for what they are, not what you interpret them to mean.

The physical and vocal information a speaker gives you, the listener, is raw data. Your job is to wait to interpret that data until you have taken the time to observe all of it. The ability to observe and describe before you interpret is at the core of appreciative listening.

3. **Be patient and ask for clarification.**

Poor listeners tend to interrupt the speaker or finish the speaker's sentences. This is arrogant and disrespectful. Such listeners assume their interpretation is correct and that the presenter need not continue. Odds are low that these listeners are 100 percent correct in their understanding. Again, look at Sara and Jerry. He not only assumes he knows what she's going to say, he doesn't even give her a chance to finish her sentence. He pounces on her words, fills in the blanks, and misinterprets what she intends to say.

Clearly, interrupting people can cause confusion, frustration, and irritation. Having said that, there are times when interrupting a speaker can save time, reduce confusion, and increase the accuracy of one's interpretation. Most speakers won't mind being interrupted if you're doing so to make sure you understand what they're saying before they go any further. More often than not, they're glad to know you're interested enough to make sure you're getting the message.

4. **Paraphrase and get confirmation.**

One of the most venerable listening skills is paraphrasing. It became popular back in the 1940s, through the work of American psychologist Carl Rogers. And while most of us know about paraphrasing, few of us have made a habit of using it.

When we paraphrase, we restate another person's message in our own words. The goal is to show that we understand it the way the presenter intends. Without paraphrasing, there is no way to know if presenter and listener are both on the same page. Actually, a listener doesn't really know if a paraphrase is accurate until the presenter says it is — this is called Confirmed Paraphrasing. Only presenters know what their intentions are. Even though their way of expressing themselves may have confused the listener, presenters remain the final judge of what they intended the listener to understand. It's one thing when people argue over what was said; it's an entirely different matter when a listener is arguing over what a presenter meant.

And it's not like paraphrasing adds that much time to the conversation — it takes the average person ten seconds or less to paraphrase. In the corporate world, those seconds could save countless hours and dollars. Case in point: I was in Belgium teaching this material to a group of executives from a global telecommunications firm. During a social hour after the session, three of the executives were discussing a major corporate decision that would come with a hefty price tag. As they started listening to each other for the first time and using their new skill of Confirmed

Paraphrasing, they realized that none of them was in favor of the decision. Collectively, they'd been ready to make the deal; but personally, each thought it was a mistake.

Cost savings: $1 million.

SUMMARY

Confirmed Paraphrasing is perhaps the most critical skill in communication. If you listen carefully, paraphrase, and get confirmation consistently, you can avoid so many communication problems. The tendency to jump to immediate interpretation can be quite costly. This is true in corporate settings, education, politics, marriage, parenting, and so on. It's time to say what we mean and mean what we say and to actually listen and accurately interpret what's being said.

Innovative InterChange requires that we listen to understand the unique thinking, valuing, and believing of another. We can come to understand only if we quit attempting to look at things only from our own perspective. We must seek to see through other lenses. To fly like an eagle, you must think like one.

Insight Questions

Personal Growth

Do you paraphrase on a consistent basis? How has it helped?

How effective are you as a listener? How could you improve?

Relationships

How do you react when people don't listen to you, when they finish your sentences, and when they misinterpret your meaning?

Why do people have a hard time listening?

Organizations

What are some areas in which your organization is effective at communication?

How could your organization be more effective, efficient, and innovative in its communication?

Chapter 16

Appreciative Understanding Tools 3 & 4

Finding Positives & Integrating Differences

Margaret didn't like what she was hearing Tim say. It felt like they were going down the same old road they'd been down so many times before. Why couldn't he just listen for once and stop lecturing?

Then she remembered something she'd learned at one of those communication effectiveness workshops — something called paraphrasing. It's worth a try, she thought. She and Tim certainly couldn't be much farther apart on this issue.

"Tim, tell me again the point you're trying to make, and let me see if I really understand what you're saying," Margaret said.

"This is new," Tim thought. "What's she up to? Is she trying to set me up?"

He answered her anyway: "I was saying I don't think we should bring on any new hires until we have cash flow to support it." He wondered how Margaret would misconstrue the message this time.

"So, what you're saying is that we should initiate a hiring freeze until we get more money in the till," Margaret said.

"Exactly!" Tim said. "That's exactly what I've been trying to tell you."

Margaret sighed. "A hiring freeze is the worst possible thing we could do right now. We're going down the tube precisely because we don't have the right people on board. Without them, we'll just continue downhill."

"Look, Margaret," Tim said. *"You can't borrow yourself rich, and the only way we can make payroll is to borrow money."*

Tim walked away from the conversation hurt and angry, and Margaret left irritated. She had paraphrased Tim, and he had even confirmed it. So what? What good did it do? They were still at odds with each other. It was clear to Margaret that the company needed some new blood to help drive revenue. Why was Tim frightened and obsessed over money while the company was going belly up, and she was offering concrete ideas for saving it?

To a certain extent, Margaret and Tim did understand each other, and at the same time, they didn't Appreciatively Understand. The point isn't that we must agree with perspectives that are different from our own. When we appreciate another person's perspective, we simply acknowledge that it has value, as much value as our own. It's pretty easy to agree with those parts of another's point of view that appear to agree with ours; the parts that clash with our version of the truth are harder for us to accept because their existence implies that we might be the one who needs to change, that our own view is limited. So, instead of being curious and wanting to learn from the differences, we prefer to eliminate them. If we can appreciate those differences, we can use them as opportunities for growth and transformation. Once again, we see how mutual respect plays into yet another aspect of Innovative InterChange.

In this chapter, we're going to talk about the two tools of the Appreciative Understanding phase: Finding Positives and Integrating Differences. With Finding Positives, you find value in another person's perspective — value that may have been obscured by your differences. When you use the Integrating Differences tool, you develop "both/and" thinking by converting *but* to *and*, and you recognize that there's enough room for diverse opinions to co-exist.

The following guideline can help you use the tool of Finding Positives:

1. Seek first the positives.

Remember that 1940s Johnny Mercer song that went, "You've got to accentuate the positive/Eliminate the negative/Latch on to the affirmative/Don't mess with Mr. In-Between"? While Appreciative Understanding isn't about ignoring so-called negatives, these lyrics do give us a clue about where to begin. Looking for positives first puts us in a more open state of mind, preparing us to deal more readily with differences of opinion later. There is value in how we sequence our response. If we start focusing immediately on what we don't like, we're more likely to end up in an argument than in an Innovative InterChange.

> **Try this exercise...** Re-read the vignette at the beginning of this chapter. What did Margaret say? What was Tim's reaction? Now, ask yourself how the conversation might have ended differently if, instead of attacking Tim's idea of a hiring freeze, Margaret had considered the idea from Tim's point of view. Put yourself in Margaret's shoes, and see if you can find at least four positive things in Tim's perspective. (For example: A hiring freeze might help control personnel costs.)

Why four positives? Some research and my experience suggest that when you invest the energy to find at least four positives in an idea you initially dislike, you tend to be less judgmental and more open to the other person's perspective. The four positives are especially helpful in potential conflict situations. As you become less judgmental, the likelihood of the other person becoming defensive decreases. Over the next thirty to sixty days, practice this idea of finding four positives as often as you can. As it becomes a habit, you'll discover a change in your attitude. You'll discover the advantage not only of understanding but also of finding value in what others say.

These next two guidelines can help you use the Integrating Differences tool:

1. Think "both/and."

A good listener seeks first to Appreciatively Understand. True appreciation is a continuum — on one end is everything we value; on the other is everything we don't. Full appreciation of anything or anyone needs to include the good, the bad, and the ugly. Appreciation is a "both/and" proposition, not just an "either/or one." It requires a change in the way we think.

What do you think when you hear the following words?

Rigid

Flexible

If you see them as contradictory, you're a victim of excessive "either/or" thinking. We do this to many words — such as *good* or *evil, right* or *wrong, black* or *white, conservative* or *liberal.* "Either/or" thinking comes from focusing on the distinctions and differences between the two words and defining them as unrelated ideas. When we look at them from a "both/and" perspective, we see them on a continuum, with many more possibilities.

Try this exercise... *Using the words rigid and flexible, write down all the positive things about being rigid that you can think of. (For example, a rigid person can provide strength.) Next, write down as many drawbacks, or so-called negatives about being rigid as you can think of. Now, think about the positives and drawbacks of being flexible. List as many of those ideas as you can think of in two minutes.*

Then, answer the following questions:

• Is a tree rigid or flexible? Which parts are rigid? Which parts are flexible? What would happen if a tree were absolutely rigid? What if it were absolutely flexible?

• *Is an airplane wing rigid or flexible? Which part is rigid? Which part is flexible? What would happen if the wing were absolutely rigid? What if it were absolutely flexible?*

• *Is a modern building in an earthquake area rigid or flexible? Is it rigid and flexible?*

• *Is the human mind rigid or flexible? Is it rigid and flexible?*

Most things in the world can be looked at from a "both/and" perspective as well as from an "either/or" perspective. Excessive "either/or" thinking often polarizes and prevents us from learning from each other; it divides families, splits politicians, and generates animosity among nations. It certainly compromises and corrupts the Innovative InterChange process. It tends to generate conflict instead of creativity. When we can integrate "either/or" with "both/and" thinking, we can diffuse potential conflicts before they start. We call this integrated way of thought "continuum" or "complementary" thinking.

2. Turn differences from obstacles into options.

Starting with the positives doesn't mean there isn't room for legitimate disagreement. It's what you do when disagreement arises that makes the difference between ending up in a conflict or an Innovative InterChange. You've probably heard the saying, "There are no problems; there are only opportunities." What you don't usually hear are people talking about how to turn problems into opportunities.

The process is really much simpler than it may seem. You start by getting back in touch with the playfulness and curiosity of your childhood. Think about how young children are always asking, "Why?"; "What if we . . .?"; "Let's pretend . . ."; "How could we . . .?"; and "I wish we . . ." This "wishful thinking" is how children leave the present and imagine an alternate reality. When we use our imagination like this, we can create a reality in which anything is possible — like turning problems into opportunities.

Often when conflict starts, it's because one person has put down or ignored another person's idea right off the bat, without even considering it. You've heard those killer statements: "That won't work!"; "It costs too much."; "We've never done it that way."; "We tried that, and it didn't work." When we say these things, we're reacting from a position of disagreement, rather than taking time to discover that there are also positives in the other person's view. Immediately rejecting what we don't like instead of taking the time to find viable options that work for everyone can waste a lot of time and energy.

> **Try this exercise...** Using the killer statements above, restate them using the "wishful thinking" statements. (For example, if the killer statement is, "We've never done it that way before," you could restate it like this: "What if we did start doing that now?" Adding "What if?" at the beginning of the statement converts it from an obstacle to a possibility.

> Now consider the Margaret and Tim story again. Keeping in mind the four positives about a hiring freeze, restate Margaret's concern about needing the right people on board, using "I wish . . .," "I wonder . . .," "How could we . . ." "What if . . .?", and "Just suppose . . ." statements. (For example, "I wish we could have the right people without bankrupting the company.")

This requires a change in thinking, which starts when we respect the other person, understand what he or she has said, find value in that perspective, and create ways to connect it to what is valuable from our own perspective. Both Margaret and Tim want the company to survive — but their strategies for doing so seem irreconcilable. They have set up their differences so that the only solution is either Tim's hiring freeze or Margaret's hiring spree because you can't have both at the same time, right? If they would work together to find a mutually supportive solution, however, they could integrate their differences by reframing the issue. The question then becomes: "How can we have the right people without bankrupting the company?" Such a way of posing it takes into consideration both perspectives.

Our journey inward requires us to change the way we think. When we can find positives and convert differences into options, our world of possibilities expands. Instead of limiting one another because of our diversity, we can expand and grow together as a result of our differences. Differences can fuel conflict or feed teamwork and community. The choice is ours.

SUMMARY

Finding Positives, the first tool of Appreciative Understanding, moves us deeper into the perspectives of both the presenter and the listener. It requires both sides to acknowledge that both points of view have equal value. From that common ground, we're more able to see positives in ideas we initially want to reject. With the second tool, Integrating Differences, we can see options instead of obstacles. The goal isn't to disregard or eliminate differences. There will always be differences. The goal is to transform how we understand, value, and use our differences for mutual support and creative growth.

Insight Questions

Personal Growth

Do you see yourself as an optimist? A pessimist? Other?

Do you say "Yes, but . . ." more often than "Yes, and . . ."?

Relationships

Is it easy for you to find value in the perspectives and ideas of others? Is this easier with some people than with others? What makes the difference?

Do you think people are more inclined to play devil's advocate or angel's advocate? How might that be changed where you live or where you work?

Organizations

Does your organization encourage you to "seek first to understand"?

A common complaint in many organizations is that management doesn't listen. Is this a problem in your organization? If so, what can you do about it?

Chapter 17

Creative Integrating Tool 5

Reframing

Simon bounded into his playroom and grabbed his friend Noah by the hand.

"C'mon, Noah! Let's go! There's a big brown bear chasing us. We have to run through the spooky, spooky forest — fast!"

The two four-year-old boys sped through the forest of dining room chairs and living room furniture, finally making it to safety in the entryway between the two front doors — squealing the entire time.

"That was a big scary bear," Simon said.

"It was very scary," Noah agreed. "What are we gonna do now?"

"We're in the elevator," Simon said. "Let's go to Saturn." And standing on tip-toe, he reached for the highest button and pushed it.

Then the two boys bent down and slowly stood up, in motion with their elevator. When the elevator stopped, Simon and Noah stepped out, into the outer space of their imagination.

Children have a natural drive to expand their world through their imagination. They're not concerned with or confined by physical boundaries like playroom walls or intangible boundaries like the laws of physics. In a child's mind, anything can be anything else —

an entryway can be an elevator to Saturn; a front porch can be a rocket ship; a bunk bed can be a train. Children make spontaneous, creative connections without any trouble at all. They're constantly asking "why," constantly exploring their environment — "What's in there?"; "What's under there?"; "What happens if you take this off?"; "What's in the drawer?" Why, what, and how questions drive our early learning.

All too soon, this world of part-fantasy, part-fact gives way to the pressure to grow up, and by the time we're adults, our minds are much less free. We've put ourselves in boxes, and we're out of practice when it comes to thinking outside of them. We've given in to cultural messages that tell us, "Grow up, and stop fooling around. Get serious!" We send those same messages to our own children when we say things like, "I don't have time to play right now. I'm working." The message is that play is something to be done after the business of life is taken care of. For awhile, our kids will keep tugging on our sleeves even though we're telling them we're too busy; they'll keep urging us to run away from the big brown bear or take a ride in the magic elevator.

Eventually, though, they get the idea that playing is for kids, and if they're going to be successful in the adult world, they have to look at life more realistically. They have to get serious. There's nothing wrong with maturing and growing up. The problem comes when we do so at the expense of spontaneity, play, imagination, and, yes, even acting silly at times. The first tool of the Creative Integrating phase, Reframing, can help you tap into your innate ability to be creative and silly, without losing the obvious advantage of being an adult who can channel that creativity into important, necessary work.

Reframing is simply about expanding your frame of reference to think about a problem, situation, or goal from a different perspective; it allows you to avoid missing ideas, options, and solutions you may never have considered.

The following strategies will be helpful as you learn how to use the Reframing tool:

1. **Let yourself go.**

The prerequisite to using Reframing is to loosen up. Don't resist your mind's natural urge to think absurd, silly, creative thoughts. Unfortunately, a number of studies over the past several decades confirm that creativity is not strong among adults. I believe it's still there — it's just dormant. The good news is, most of us are fully capable of reactivating our imaginations; we just have to quit listening to those messages in our self talk that say, "Don't act silly," "I can't imagine that," and "I'm not very creative." You can rediscover playful work and productive play. Telling yourself that you're not creative reduces your openness to being creative. Give yourself permission to be silly; allow for the possibility that the random, spontaneous thoughts that come when you play are connected on some level — this is important for integrating differences that on the surface appear to be mutually exclusive.

The challenge for many adults is to perceive the value in rediscovering their imaginations. We have a hard time believing that imagination has a practical side. The truth is, imagination is at the very core of creativity and innovation. It's basic to becoming more fully who we are capable of being. It's the eagle's willingness to imagine what it would be like to fly high in the sky that arouses his urge to soar. Remember that Einstein said, "Imagination is more important than reason." The imagination is the door to changing our minds, shifting our paradigms, thinking outside the box, integrating differences, and putting the innovation in Innovative InterChange.

2. **Don't jump to solutions.**

In the Innovative InterChange process, imagination comes into play once we've discovered and appreciatively understood the similarities and differences in multiple perspectives. This is the point at which it can seem like all the appreciation in the world won't help us reconcile our differences. In the story about Tim and Margaret in Chapter 16, it appears absurd to think that a hiring freeze and hiring new people could be compatible. But with a little imagination, they can be. Look at the broader motivations here: Tim is ultimately concerned with fiscal responsibility, and Margaret wants a skilled workforce. Suddenly, the two ideas don't seem so mutually exclusive, do they? Now integrating the two of them can start to imagine scenarios in which employees are helping to increase revenue, not drain it.

The key to Reframing is to avoid jumping immediately to solutions and assuming that only one perspective can be right. The more ways we can look at an issue or problem, the better. Too often, people end up in arguments over how to solve a problem instead of first stepping back and reconsidering the problem from different angles.

Einstein said, "Our present problems cannot be solved at the level of thinking at which they were created." He meant we'll get nowhere unless we look at issues from multiple angles, even using different words to describe them. Reframing an issue can open us up to fresh, novel, and creative possibilities we'd never discover otherwise.

> **Try this exercise...** How do you state a problem, frame an issue, or describe a circumstance in different ways and from different perspectives? Let's take Tim and Margaret's dilemma and think about the problem of declining revenue. Focus on the word *declining*. Being as spontaneous as you can, let pictures, images, ideas, and feelings come naturally, and write them down as they occur to you. (For example, you might imagine a balloon getting smaller — declining in volume — as the air flows out. Or you might picture a loaf of freshly baked bread that has fallen — declined in height — after you've taken it out of the oven.)

Now, Reframe the problem of declining revenue based on one of the images that came to you. Write down as many Reframed statements as you can think of. (For example, using the images of the deflated balloon and the fallen bread, you might say, "I wish we could take the excess inflation out of the budget" or "Suppose we could add enough dough and yeast to prevent the budget from falling.")

Seemingly random ideas and images can be very practical, even critical, when you're problem-solving. Seeing and using things in new ways doesn't deny or detract from their original design and purpose. You're simply expanding their use. The entryway in Simon's house is still a place to take off wet boots, even as Simon transforms it in his mind into an elevator to Saturn.

Fantasy doesn't negate fact, and fact doesn't have to negate fantasy. We can have them both. We can fly like an eagle and still know what it's like to run around the chicken yard. Our eagle will know things no conventional eagle will ever know. He's never been like any other chicken, but now he's beginning to Appreciatively Understand why he's no ordinary eagle, either.

SUMMARY

The Reframing tool of Creative Integrating is more than Appreciative Understanding. It's about all parties letting go of their own ways of looking at an issue and using their imaginations to redefine it, to pry open their narrow ways of thinking. By mixing fantasy and fact, sense and nonsense, we free our minds from encrusted habitual ways of thinking about things, others, and ourselves. It allows the fresh air of new ideas to alter how we perceive, think, and create. In short, if you want to end at a different place, start from one.

Insight Questions

Personal Growth

Do you have thoughts that run through your head that tell you not to act silly?

Do you tend to use your imagination to conjure up positive outcomes? Do you imagine worst-case scenarios?

Relationships

Do you think most people can be creative? Do you think only a few are born that way?

How can people encourage others to use their imagination?

Organizations

Does your organization encourage you to think outside the box? Does it provide you with the tools and opportunity to do so?

Does your company's management think there can ever be too much creativity? Do you?

Chapter 18

Creative Integrating Tool 6

Reconfiguring

About 35 people from two divisions of a major company were gathered for an Innovative Interchange session. Both groups had been through a prior session to learn techniques for engaging in Authentic Interacting and Appreciative Understanding and recapturing their openness and curiosity. The two divisions had been rivals for more than 30 years — competing over budgets, questioning each other's competence, and vying to set the goals for the company. The groups seldom got together, except as part of larger company-wide meetings. But the Innovative InterChange workshop had prepared each division to arrive at this session with an air of curiosity rather than caution and suspicion. The objective was to build on what they'd already learned and develop ways to be more collaborative and innovative.

The two-day session was lively, playful even. People let their guards down and threw every idea they had on the table — the wackier, the better. No one scoffed. There were no arguments about whose ideas were better or which ones would never work. Everyone just let their imaginations run wild. Everyone had fun.

When they were finished, they realized they had generated many more creative ideas together than they would have working alone. So they decided they would request a joint budget from the corporate office and set up a common meeting space so they could work together and share ideas on a continual basis.

It's been said that if you want a good idea, you need to have lots of them. One way to do that is to bring lots of minds and imaginations together. And whether you're in a group or by yourself, the freshest ideas come when you let them occur to you spontaneously. Unfortunately, most of us stem the flow of ideas because we think they must be complete and perfect before they're worth thinking about or sharing. We tend to be far too serious about our thinking. Being serious is important — and so is playfulness, especially when it comes to problem-solving. We need to not only let the ideas come freely, we need to turn them over to see what's on the flip side and look inside to see how they're put together. By closely examining, rearranging, and integrating ideas in our imaginations, we work our way out of our mental and emotional boxes. We calm our aversion to absurdity.

After we've Reframed an issue or problem to trigger ideas we wouldn't have thought of otherwise, the next step is to use the second tool of Creative Integrating, Reconfiguring. When you Reconfigure, you play and use your imagination; you step away from your problem, situation, or goal completely and use metaphors and outside-the-box thinking to generate new ideas. This moves us from our comfort zone to our creative zone. Instead of immediately judging a new idea as good or bad, when we're in the creative zone we can make any idea more relevant.

Below are some guidelines we can use in Reconfiguring:

1. **Go to the "twilight zone."**

When we Reconfigure an idea, we break it up into pieces and connect it with other ideas to form a hybrid. Such hybrid ideas can be part fantasy and part fact, part familiar and part unfamiliar, part serious and part humorous, part practical and part nonsensical. Creativity and innovation are about making connections, lots of connections. The connections initially don't have to be practical or even doable. They just need to be allowed to rub up against each other for awhile. This is difficult when you feel you must have perfect ideas the first time, every time. Be willing to accept that everything and anything can be connected, no matter how far apart the ideas may seem to be at first. Be willing to embrace the ambiguity in your mind during the early phases of the creative process. Things don't have to make sense at first in order to become relevant and useful later.

Think of this early phase as a "twilight zone." This zone superimposes the comfort and creative zones. Most of us have experienced such a zone in our dreams. When you dream, you give yourself permission to defy gravity, to run without moving, to swim underwater without scuba equipment. In dreams, your mind plays with ideas, stretches your reality like a rubber band. It brings together things that on the surface would have no business being connected — like a penguin playing pool or George Washington playing an electric guitar.

There's a reason your mind does this, and there's a reason it happens while you're sleeping. We seem to be designed to work in the creative zone — it's the seat of our originality. And when we dream, our mind is free to go where it needs to go. When we're awake, we're much more in control; we stay in our comfort zone most of the time because it makes sense, it feels right, it seems safe. Ideally, we'd move seamlessly in and out of our creative zone with greater regularity. It's the place where we can generate new ideas.

If the old eagle had rejected all of his thoughts about flying, he would've remained in the confines of the backyard. Instead, he was open to his urges, thoughts, and imaginings. He was open to expanding beyond his comfort zone and embracing his creative zone. He had to think like an eagle if he were ever going to learn to fly like one.

2. **Think metaphorically.**

What's really happening when you're in your twilight zone — certainly when you're sleeping — is that you're thinking and imagining in metaphor, simile, and analogy. You're Reconfiguring your reality for awhile. You're bridging the gap between fantasy and fact, familiarity and the unfamiliar.

> **Try this exercise — Part I...** Think of an issue or a problem you're having and write down all of the images that come to mind when you think about the problem.
>
> For example, you might ask yourself, "How can I stop people from coming into my office and disrupting what I'm doing?" Images that could come to mind are an asteroid heading toward Earth's path, threatening to disrupt the entire planet; a jack-in-the-box jumping through its lid; or a frog's tongue darting out to grab a passing insect.

You probably notice obvious parallels between these images and the idea of someone bursting into your office unannounced — particularly the similarities between sudden movement in the images and the sudden movement of the person interrupting you.

What may be less obvious is how we can use these images to stimulate original and creative thinking. It's less obvious because we're not used to letting spontaneous thoughts emerge and then looking for ways to connect them; we confine our thinking to the immediate situation. In the case of people coming through our door unexpectedly, we tend to stay focused on the idea of a door and the familiar faces coming through it. Sticking with that narrow image, we're likely to come up with typical solutions, such as locking the door so they can't come in or doing our work elsewhere so we won't be there when people come to interrupt.

Of course, there's nothing inherently wrong with typical solutions. The problem is, we may be missing even more creative, long-lasting answers. Rational and logical thought without the spontaneity of creative thought tends to keep us right where we are, doing what we've always done, and wondering why we keep getting the same results.

Try this exercise — Part II... Go back to your issue, and pick one of the images or ideas from your list and generate as many Reconfigured ideas as you can think of.

For example, let's continue with the issue of people coming through the office door, and let's pick the image of an asteroid headed toward Earth. It is important at this point to put some distance between you and the actual problem by shifting your thinking and imaginatively and playfully exploring another world. In this case, you would forget about doors and people interrupting for awhile and let your mind wander around the world of astronomy and astrophysics. You might think about stray asteroids passing through our solar system unannounced from time to time, causing major disruption. They say the craters on the moon were caused by such collisions, and there is evidence that asteroids once hit Earth with great frequency. Perhaps you'd start thinking about those movies in which the hero has to find a way to divert or destroy a killer asteroid before it destroys the world.

Now you'd use the *I wish ...* and *Suppose ...* phrases we discussed in Chapter 16 to see if asteroids can generate any ideas for reducing the number of people who come through the office door and interrupt you:

I wish I had some sort of early detection process that would warn me of an impending interruption.

What if I could I divert the interrupter's path before she enters mine?

Suppose I could destroy the reason someone wants to see me?

Suppose I'm interrupted only when I want to be?
How can I make interruptions fun?

Playing with the idea of asteroids allows you to Reconfigure your problem. "Making interruptions fun" could be a far more interesting notion than just locking people out of your office. And you may never have thought of it if you hadn't gotten outside the comfort of your conventional way of thinking.

Now, choose a Reconfigured idea from your list and imagine a way to make it work in your life or work.

For example, in the list of sample Reconfigured statements above, you could focus on the idea of an early warning system. You could start your day by visiting the people who interrupt you most often and asking them if there are any issues they might need your help with. This will let them know that you work more effectively if you can plan for contingencies, and it sends the message that you support their work. You can also tell them that unless it's an emergency, they can simply send you an e-mail about their issue, and you will let them know when it's convenient for you to talk. With just a quick check-in, you can get control of some of the minor interruptions in your schedule.

Some say that in order to be creative we must live in some sort of tension. Perhaps — but the tension doesn't have to stress us out. We get stressed when we lock ourselves away in comfort while our creative self is banging at our door. We must be willing to trust that we will find satisfaction if we open the door to creative transformation.

SUMMARY

The Reconfiguring tool of Creative Integrating is the bridge between being and becoming, between current reality and our dreams. We use it to mix fact and fantasy to create new possibilities and opportunities. But in order to do it well, we need to be willing to play with the absurd, think in metaphoric terms, and become comfortable with ambiguity.

We can embrace the good, the bad, and the ugly to create something beautiful. It's sort of thinking like *Beauty and the Beast*. Each can find the best and invent around the rest. The adult in us must integrate with our child within so we can let go of our inhibitions, experience continuous learning. By letting our brains generate and playfully connect ideas, we experience the satisfaction of our originality. We have to let any old (or new) idea into our heads, no matter how silly or crazy it may seem to our normal way of thinking. Quit prejudging what value or meaning your ideas have at first glance.

The old eagle can be one up on his new eagle neighbors because he knows what's inside a chicken's mind. There are surely things from chicken technology that can be useful to a late-blooming eagle. If he outright rejects his thoughts about flying, he will stay in the backyard. Instead he is open to his urges, thoughts, and daydreams.

Insight Questions

Personal Growth

How can you let go of your inhibition to act silly? How can you let your imagination flow?

A good sense of humor is useful in freeing the imagination. How would you rate your sense of humor? What might you do to expand it?

Relationships

Do your friends encourage you to have fun and act silly at times? How do you feel when you risk acting in a less mature fashion?

Think about your friends. Are they more creative or more conforming?

Organizations

Is imagination a priority in your organization?

Is your organization able to think in terms of playful work and productive play? Give examples.

Chapter 19

Continual Transforming Tools 7 & 8

Repeating & Observing and Positive Reinforcing & Correcting

It was late summer before our eagle got into the full swing of practicing his flying skills. He started out doing exercises to strengthen his wings and running laps around the backyard to increase his stamina and speed.

Then it was time to put the two together.

So he moved to the farthest corner of the backyard, took a deep breath, focused his attention, and began to run as fast as he could. When he was two-thirds of the way across the yard, he leaped as high as he could and began to flap his wings as hard as he could. For a moment, he lifted off the ground, his strong wings pressed against the air. Then, he lost his balance and brushed the edge of the garage, crashing headlong into the garbage can and spilling trash everywhere. His right wing and chest were covered with coffee grounds, and part of a banana peel had wrapped itself around his left leg. It might have been funny if it weren't for the

*pain emanating from the top of his head, which had scraped the
ground as he careened off the garbage can lid.*

*It was a start, not the start he imagined, but a start nonetheless.
It was a moment of decision. He was tempted to call the whole
thing off. He could admit that chickens are indeed creatures of the
ground. He could tell himself he was too old for such foolishness.
But he didn't choose either of those options. Instead, he took it as
a sign that he needed more than intent, courage, wing strength,
and stamina. He realized he needed practice, practice, and
more practice to coordinate his ambition with his developing
aerodynamics.*

*So, day after day, he practiced in his mind and with his body
— until one afternoon, it happened. He started from the corner of
the yard, as always, and began to flap hard and jump high. Before
he knew it, he had taken off. He was flying! From the tips of his
wings to the tips of his claws, from the point of his beak to the end
of his tail, he was flying. No — not just flying. He was flying like an
eagle. He was realizing his dream. He was satisfying his urge, and
he was actualizing his destiny. He had reached the sky.*

Indeed, it's hard to learn something new and look good while
you're learning. Learning is awkward. It has its ups and downs,
successes and failures. It's a cycle of trial-success-error-correction.
The glue of such learning is commitment, dedication, discipline,
and perseverance. It's the function of intention, action, repetition,
attention, correction, and perspiration. The journey to the original
self is no different. We must want it badly enough to withstand the
awkward moments and the bumps and bruises.

There are two tools in the Continual Transforming phase of
Innovative InterChange: Repeating & Observing and Positive
Reinforcing & Correcting. These tools are primarily about choices

and discipline. They're about being willing to expand the way you are in order to let go of the habits that prevent you from becoming more of who you can be.

The following strategies will help you use these tools:

1. **Focus on specific results.**

Remember what Stephen Covey advised: "Begin with the end in mind." In mastering Innovative InterChange, you need to have a clear understanding of the six primary tools and skills. You may not have mastered them, but hopefully you've at least tried some of them. Now it's time to turn these skills into habits. To begin, it helps to know what it will look like when you have mastered the process — it helps to know what you intend to do:

• Authentically Interact by sharing the best you know with integrity, and have clear intentions for what and how you want to inform others.

• Appreciatively Understand by listening with humility to what others think, and be curious about their unique perspectives; paraphrase what you understand another person's message to be and wait for confirmation.

• Find Hidden Positives in the perspectives of others.

• Integrate Difference by using "both/and" thinking.

• Reframe issues, differences, and problems in order to discover better ways to integrate differences and to find creative solutions.

• Use your imagination to Reconfigure and reconnect ideas, metaphors, images, and analogies to create new perspectives and opportunities for action.

2. **Make a commitment.**

There's an old story about a hen and a pig who were watching a farmer eat breakfast. The pig was proud of the swine contribution of bacon and sausage. The hen was boasting about how chickens provided the eggs. The pig was quick to point out that the chicken's contribution was one of involvement in providing eggs, while the pig's contribution required a total commitment to provide ham and sausage. In short, the hen walked away, while the pig remained on the platter. Commitment involves a cost, while involvement can cost little or nothing.

Intentions don't go far without commitment. Many of us need support in order to follow through on our good intentions. Commitment depends on how much we value the goal toward which we're working. How much is being your original self worth? How much would you pay? How far would you go? Being our original self takes courage, patience, and perseverance.

3. **Practice — a lot.**

You can't master anything of substance without practice. The more you repeat the tools and skills of Innovative InterChange, the more natural they will feel — repetitions rewire and strengthen the synapses in your brain. It may take thirty, sixty, ninety days or more, and some days you'll do well, while other days, you'll fall into old habits. The key is to accept your setbacks and mistakes, get up, and do it again, and again, and again until you get where you intended to go. While repetition is critical, it's not the whole story. If you practice something incorrectly, you'll master doing it incorrectly. You must use the correct tools and behaviors.

4. **Observe and remember.**

Have you ever had a good intention, but then you forgot to follow through? To make a new skill into a habit, you have to be a good observer — and observation is about remembering to keep your attention on your intention. Your existing habits tend to be automatic and unconscious; learning something new requires extra attention and a conscious effort.

Be willing to go to extremes to ensure you remember to practice. Post sticky notes everywhere if you have to — on your computer, stair railing, mirror, or steering wheel. Put them on objects you know you will have to pick up before you go out, like your wallet, car keys, or money. Put reminders in your PDA and your computer; create tickler files; ask your friends to e-mail you with reminders or call you to meet for coffee to discuss your progress. There are hundreds of ways to remember — as long as you remember to use them.

5. **Celebrate your successes.**

When you catch yourself doing it right, reward yourself! Celebration will keep you going during the tough parts later. In our culture, people tend to call our attention to our mistakes and failures. It's a subtle, yet important, distinction.

Instead of focusing on your mistakes and how you can avoid them, catch yourself doing something right. It feels a whole lot better. And that satisfaction is the best reward there is. Of course, it's okay to treat yourself sometimes, too — maybe a bowl of ice cream, a day at the spa, or an afternoon at the park. Whatever your pleasure.

6. **Correct your mistakes.**

If you do catch yourself doing something you did not intend to do, don't beat yourself up. Simply notice that you've gotten off track a little, and use your imagination to discover other ways to remind yourself of your commitment.

Negative thinking actually increases the probability that you'll make the same mistake again, get discouraged, and search for reasons to give up and revert to old habits. Acknowledging an error is one thing; dwelling on it and punishing yourself for it only adds insult to injury. So stay positive and focused on your goal. Dwell on the result you intend rather than the mistakes you make along the way. Celebration encourages, correction improves, and together they reward your commitment.

The bottom line

So what's the payoff for all this effort? Being and becoming our original creative self, of course. It's the highest level of satisfaction we can reach. It won't erase the tragedies of life, heal our illnesses, end war, or prevent death. It will pull us beyond our narrow and trivial selves. It opens the door to self-transformation as well as meaningful relationships, collaboration, teamwork, and community. Some people think their highest satisfaction is in arriving at a destination — a heaven, a nirvana, a final resting place. Other people believe satisfaction is in the journey itself. I believe it's in both. The original self and the created self are arriving and leaving, beginning and ending all the time.

Two-fold commitment

The original self and the created self can become integrated into a whole self that is both being and becoming. You can be a chicken and an eagle. You don't have to be someone else at the expense of your original self, and you don't have to become a hermit to maintain your unique identity. It's when people Authentically Interact with each other that their distinctiveness is broadened. We can experience our individuality in community and community in our individuality.

To integrate our self and become mutually supportive of others who are being their original selves, we must practice a two-fold commitment. It isn't enough to be committed to being and doing our best without being open to change, growth, and transformation. It isn't sufficient to be committed to ongoing learning and transformation if we're unwilling to be and act on the best we are and know.

Living this two-fold commitment consistently brings us life's greatest satisfaction and fulfills our highest destiny, to be all any of us can be and become. It frees us to leave the backyard to soar to ever-greater heights in a cloudless sky.

Insight Questions

Personal Growth

In what ways are you a disciplined person? Do you follow through on your commitments?

How would you explain the two-fold commitment to others? Give examples.

Relationships

If your friends were to describe you, would they have an accurate understanding of who you are? Are there parts of yourself you seldom, if ever, share? Why?

Do you engage in Innovative InterChange on a regular basis?

Organizations

Does your organization provide opportunities for you to be and do your best?

Does your organization provide opportunities for you to become more of who you are capable of being and becoming?

Innovative InterChange
Conditions, Phases, Skills & Tools

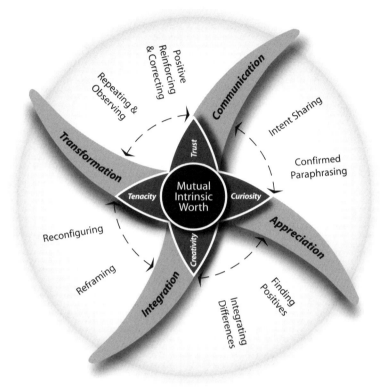

In Part III, you learned the eight thinking tools and behavioral skills that can help you engage more consistently in Innovative InterChange, which can help you find the satisfaction you seek. With Intent Sharing and Confirmed Paraphrasing, you can make your communication more authentic and productive. Finding Positives and Integrating Differences expand your frame of reference and allow you to find and appreciate possibilities in ideas that you may have judged to be obstacles. Reframing and Reconfiguring leverage your ability to integrate and imagine new ways of thinking about issues and solving problems. Finally, Repeating & Observing and Positive Reinforcing & Correcting are the tools that help you make the whole process a habit. They help you change your behavior and your thought process for good.

Epilogue

It was nearly that moment when day and night embrace. The sun was drifting low in the western sky, painting the edges of the clouds pink. A lone eagle winged its way through the air. He studied the ground below for rodents that had carelessly strayed too far from a safe haven. The old eagle remembered earlier times when he had settled for corn and insects to silence a ravenous appetite that never seemed quite satisfied. It would be his last catch of the day. Suddenly, from the corner of his eye, he caught a glimpse of something else, something not on the ground but descending from high above. It seemed almost translucent in the dying rays of the setting sun. It moved in absolute silence. A strange sensation filled his body.

This stranger from the heavens was kindling a response in him that was reminiscent of the urge he first felt when he saw the eagle soaring over his former backyard home, but this was no eagle. This was a bird of a different feather, if indeed it had feathers. It was like he was seeing himself, but not as an eagle. He had been a chicken of sorts and now an eagle, but this new urge was calling him beyond both. What he heard was startling. He could have sworn the strange bird said something — and it seemed to be coming from within and beyond. The strange bird said, "Let me fly for you. Let go, and let me." That was all. In the next instant, it was gone.

The eagle searched the sky in all directions, frantically looking for the mysterious bird. Nothing. All that was left were a few pink-tipped clouds and a strange sensation near his heart, like wings gently flapping. In an instant he knew — knew that becoming his true original self wasn't his final destination. It was his starting point.

Dr. Charlie Palmgren worked for 40 years as an international consultant to top management at such corporations as Microsoft, Motorola, and Accenture (formerly Arthur Andersen). He has spent decades researching and writing about organizational development, human behavior, and human transformation, among other subjects. His professional experience also includes roles as a personal and family counselor, drug prevention program director, medical school professor, and leader of public education reform in the White House initiative "Communities in Schools."

Before helping to start Innovative InterChange Associates in Dayton, Ohio, Dr. Palmgren co-founded SynerChange International, Inc., an Atlanta-based consulting firm based on the principles of Innovative InterChange.

Dr. Palmgren earned his Ph.D. in applied behavior science and organizational development from Union Institute and University. He holds bachelor's and master's degrees in psychology and a bachelor's degree in philosophy from Drake University; he also has done graduate work in psychiatry and alcoholism.

He lives in Nashville, Tennessee, with his wife, Marian.

Innovative InterChange

What we do

Innovative InterChange is a consulting and coaching company, offering customized, in-depth communication and leadership skills development for groups and individuals who want to restructure the habits that prevent creative, authentic interaction. We provide a framework of skills and tools to help people reach their highest potential for being productive, collaborative, and innovative. We don't offer quick tips or checklists for managing a few challenges. We coach people toward "Aha" moments that transform their personal and professional lives. We align ourselves with our clients as partners to assist them in achieving their goals and objectives and we stick with them to help make their new skills a habit.

How we got here

Innovative InterChange was founded in 2006 by Kathy and Frank Hollingsworth and Dr. Charlie and Marian Palmgren. The Hollingsworths and Dr. Palmgren met in 2004, after decades in other professions — Kathy in banking, Frank in information technology and project management, and Charlie in behavioral science, corporate consulting, and Episcopal ministry.

What we offer

Group workshops
Group and individual coaching
Organizational retreats
Leadership development

Books available

The Chicken Conspiracy
Ascent of the Eagle

For more information

email info@iiChange.com
Log on to www.InnovativeInterChange.com